Midnight Run

My Narrow Escape to a Better Future

by

Kevin Honeycutt

and

Terri Peckham

Midnight Run

Acknowledgements

I have so many people to thank for their support and encouragement in my life and with the completion of this book. A simple thank you to my mother seems so inadequate. My quest to make her proud resulted in all of the success that I've had. Thank you, Mom, for being you and for protecting this creative, sensitive kid from so many bad things.

Thanks to my friend, Terri. Your wit, wisdom and creativity have made this book possible.

Thanks to my beautiful wife, Michele. Everything I am or will be was purchased by your love.

Thanks to my son, Benjamin, for inspiring me daily. Your writing and drive to write have made me want to do the same.

Thanks to my new little boy, Gibson. Your arrival has made me young again. The future I see in your eyes drives me to be there to see as much of it as possible.

About the Author

Kevin Honeycutt is a nationally recognized speaker on a variety of topics dealing with student engagement, technology integration, and change in schools.

Kevin is married to Michele Honeycutt and they have two sons—Ben and Gibson. In addition to being an inspirational speaker and passionate teacher, Kevin is an artist, musician, and dedicated school board member.

Kevin is often on the road so his free time is spent enjoying the company of family and friends, but he also finds time to drive his beloved Camaro. Becoming a father for the second time at the age of 48 has been a transformational experience!

Preface

As you dive into this book, please note that these are simple stories written with my voice and transposed and edited by a talented, brilliant and funny woman named Terri. None of this would be possible without her. Additionally, I want you to know that if you're expecting a novel or anything recognizable as a regular book, you're apt to be confused. It's best to just relax, sit back and let this happen to you. Thanks for taking a little time to see and, hopefully, learn from my journey.

Kevin Honeycutt

Introduction

Midnight Run is the story of my life. I guess more specifically it is mainly the story of my childhood and early adult years. The stories I share are very personal and told from my perspective. I've verified some of the early dates and places with my mother, but the events are told from my recollection. Just as the blind men who were feeling different parts of an elephant described a very different creature, my siblings or other family members might have viewed these same experiences through a different lens.

My intent is not to indict or vilify anyone. I'm telling my story, my way in the hope that anyone going through a similar experience might benefit from the lessons I learned that helped me build a better life. If you find any of the stories poignant or emotional, I ask that you use those feelings to help others you might encounter who are struggling in life because everyone deserves a chance to make a "midnight run" to a brighter future.

Midnight Run

The story of my life isn't significantly different from that of many others. My life was filled with good moments and bad, but growing up with an alcoholic father who was also an occasional con man and an outlaw, there were more bad experiences than good ones. When I incorporate my story into my presentations, people often ask me, "How did you overcome such a difficult start in life and become a successful adult?" The answer is that I was able to take away something positive every time, and I want to share those lessons learned and how I used them to build a life. I want to share them because I hope others in similar circumstances can use the things I learned to find their way out just like I did. I truly believe that the best way out of darkness is to make your own light. Again, I realize there are countless others out there who had it just as rough, if not rougher, than I did growing up, but as a trainer and motivational speaker, I have a larger venue to share my experiences. One experience that left an indelible mark on me was the Midnight Run.

"Midnight run" was all Dad had to say, and everyone in my family knew what to do. We each got a trash bag, the Honeycutt version of luggage, and we packed our most prized possessions inside. Anything that wouldn't fit in the trash bag was left behind, no matter how dear it might be to the owner. We couldn't say our good-byes to friends because no one could know that we were leaving. Under cover of darkness, the seven of us would squeeze into whatever vehicle Dad had at the time, sometimes it was a pickup, and disappear into the night.

Several things could trigger a midnight run, but it usually occurred when Dad owed so much money to individuals and businesses that he could no longer get credit anywhere in the town. So we would leave without paying those debts and try to make a fresh start somewhere, anywhere. Sometimes we had a destination, and sometimes we left without a clue as to where we were headed. I remember seeing so many signs in the moonlight that said, "Leaving Anywhere, USA," and I tried to memorize the names of each place. I had the childish dream that someday I would go back to each of those towns and pay back the money Dad owed. It took me a long time to accept the fact that the sins of the father aren't passed on to the son, and neither are his debts. However, I believe that my commitment to making the world a better place is an attempt to settle those old accounts.

The biggest residual effect of our nomadic lifestyle was the lack of long-term relationships. It was hard to invest in a friendship that you knew from the start wasn't going to last. As an adult, it took time to learn how to cultivate those relationships and trust that the people I connected with could be in my life permanently. Building strong, lasting relationships and surrounding myself with people who helped build me up has been a major step in making my own Midnight Run to a brighter future.

Seasoned Green Oak

If you have any experience burning wood, you can probably picture nights you spent in front of a crackling fire surrounded by loved ones. If you don't have experience burning wood, you may not know that seasoned wood and green wood are opposites, and green wood doesn't burn well. Instead of crackling and providing warmth, it smokes up the entire house. There's no way wood can be seasoned and green at the same time so I'll explain what the phrase "seasoned green oak" means to me.

I used to sell "seasoned green oak" when I was young, and that activity was indicative of the way I spent my entire childhood. As I said, my dad was a con man who always looked for the easy way out of everything, and the way we sold firewood was a perfect example. Dad would send us out from the relative warmth of whatever ramshackle truck he had procured to knock on doors. We learned to be salesmen in the freezing winter in Pennsylvania, and that was a great motivator. Our pay at the end of the night, if we were successful, was a hotlink sandwich (think poor man's Panini) and a hot cocoa from a convenience store along the way. The sooner we made a sale, the sooner we could get out of the cold, but God forbid we made a sale too quickly because that would trigger the dreaded second load scenario. A quick sale meant we would hurry home, grab a second load, and start the whole process again.

If we knocked on doors all night without finding a buyer, Dad would implement the Sob Story. The Sob Story started with a drive to an affluent neighborhood where Dad unhooked the truck's wiring harness to make the vehicle appear disabled. With the hood raised and Dad banging his tools loudly, it wasn't long before the locals would investigate the commotion. The story we shared with the good citizens once they left their warm homes was that Dad needed to sell this load of wood so he could afford to call for a tow truck and get these poor, cold children home. Much of this was true because we were definitely poor and cold and we weren't going anywhere until the wood was sold. The Sob Story seldom failed us, and once Dad closed the deal, he would lead us into the house to make the fake call to the wrecker service. Inside I smelled the wondrous scents of flower arrangements, new carpet, and warm dinners. I always thought this was how rich people's houses smelled. Once we closed the deal, Dad would hook up the wiring harness, and we'd be on our way. The Sob Story alone was bad enough, but that was only a small part of the scam.

Dad always seemed able to find somebody who would let him clear wood, and he would cut down live trees with green leaves and sap, certainly nothing suitable for burning. He would cut them down, split the wood, and throw it in the truck. He always kept a small supply of seasoned wood that had been cut the year before so it had time to dry sufficiently. He would put that on top so it covered the green wood below. This was a veneer, a cosmetic veneer. Then we would go door to door, and the people would come out to look at the wood we had for sale. Obviously, we hoped and prayed they wouldn't lift more than one piece to see the green wood that would burn poorly and probably smoke up their house. In cases where we snared a customer, Dad would talk to them at length around front as we kids stacked the green wood, placed the seasoned oak back in the truck, and neatly wrapped the stack of wood in Dad's trademark complimentary black plastic, ensuring prying eyes wouldn't see that it was green until well after our clean getaway.

Once our home phone rang, and the person on the other end was an angry firewood customer. He explained that he had tried to light our product with a blowtorch without luck. Dad yelled, "How did you get this number," and he quickly slammed down the receiver. With no actual business number to contact, disgruntled customers rarely tracked him down so we ran our scam with virtual impunity.

Being a salesman is an honorable profession if it's done ethically, but Dad taught us how to sell a bad product, how to cheat people. We had to do that. That was part of being a kid in our house. We were making the money to pay the bills and put food on the table, but that didn't make me feel any better about what I was doing. Instead of accepting my Dad's example as the path I would follow, I chose to overcome that adversity. I began to think of life as a game of Plinko, and I was dropping, bouncing, and hitting things all the way down. The difference between Plinko and the Game of Life was that my path wasn't ruled by chance or gravity. At every turn, I had a choice, and I decided that I didn't want to sell things that weren't real.

Dad taught us that it's important to be out there, to knock on doors and look for opportunity, but what I learned on my own was the importance of selling something that is genuine and sustainable. You can get away with ripping people off; you can do that for a little while, but not for long. You know eventually it's going to come back and get you. But if you're sharing something you really believe in, you can leave the past behind and find the life you were meant to live.

No Shortcuts

For most people living in poverty, the true social safety net is family. If you are experiencing extreme hardship, you find a family member who is doing just a little better than you are, and you ask for help. This happened to us frequently, and in 1979, my Aunt Gladys was our safety net. When we needed help, we didn't live with people; we lived on people. We always used the word living "on" people rather than living "off" people. It's a subtle difference, but in my mind "on" suggested help from a family member that was given freely, whereas "off" implied taking advantage of someone or mooching. We would move in with somebody temporarily (supposedly a week or two), but it would turn into a year. As a result of overstaying our welcome, there would be arguments, and we would have to move out quickly. That's exactly what happened when we had to leave Aunt Gladys' house and go to Woodbine, Maryland.

An old friend of Dad's found us a house so he probably got us in rent-free. I remember how happy we were moving in that first night. We finally had a place to call our own after all that time spent with Aunt Gladys. Mom was setting up the whatnots—the stuff she took from town to town that made home seem like home. She only had a handful of these things, but there was some normalcy in the fact that you saw the same artifacts in every house. Dad had been sober for a while, but once he thought everything was okay, he would drink again. Now that he'd suddenly found a house for the family to live in, it was time to celebrate. He cracked the top on a cold one and started back into his old routine. Mom, in the meantime, didn't know he'd started drinking again.

The start of his drinking binges always put a lot of stress on me. I was always the kid who told on him, not because I was a turncoat or a bad guy. I just didn't want Mom to be blindsided by reality when she thought everything was going well. It broke my heart to see that happen so I often told on him, and he got really mad at me for that. He thought I was the worst kind of person, but I just couldn't stand to see Mom destroyed when the inevitable realization hit her. I knew she was the fabric that held the family together so I tried to protect her as best I could.

Whenever Dad started drinking, I got scared because I knew anything could happen. On this particular evening, it was very cold in the house. It was late fall, but it was already cold. You could see your breath in the house, and we didn't have the money to turn on the gas. However, early that morning Dad did what he had done his entire life; he took a shortcut by finding a tool he could use to turn the gas on himself. What he didn't know was that the furnace was missing a fitting so gas was filling the basement the entire day.

You can probably imagine exactly what happened next, but I'll set the scene. Everything is almost in order, and Mom is happy that the house is starting to look like a home again. The rest of us are unpacking our meager belongings. My sister, who has just gotten out of the bathtub, is wrapped in a towel with her arms, legs and hair wet. She is standing by Dad at the top of the stairs when he flips the switch to start the furnace. This happy scene will always be juxtaposed in my memory with the devastation that followed in the next instant.

When Dad flipped the switch, the house exploded. It was such a violent explosion that it blew the house off the foundation. It threw Dad and my sister back against the wall. None of the rest of us were seriously injured, but we were disoriented and scattered around the house by the force of the blast. As we regained our senses, we gathered together outside the house one by one.

Ambulances and fire trucks arrived on the scene. I wish I could say this was exciting, but this was normal in my family. Emergency vehicles showed up at least once a month. I met up with my sister, Sandy, who had been nearest to dad at the time of the explosion. As I moved beside her where she sat on the ground, she said, "Hold me." This was almost as big a shock as the explosion. Even though my sister was a year younger, I perceived that she was superior to me in every way so I couldn't imagine that she was turning to me for comfort. I reached down to pick her up, and when I put my arms around her, her skin stuck to my arms.

Even as a child, I realized she was in bad shape. She was in total shock and didn't feel anything at the time so that was a blessing. An emergency helicopter was flown in to take her to the Baltimore City Burn Unit where she was diagnosed with 3rd degree burns on 75% of her body. Dad had some burns, but Sandy was the most seriously injured person by far.

Sandy spent many days in the burn unit, but eventually she made a full recovery. This experience taught me how dangerous it can be to take a shortcut. If Dad had paid his bill and contacted the gas company, they would have sent someone out to inspect the line and turn on the gas. There was no reason for all the pain and suffering to ever happen, but dad took the shortcut.

In all our lives we have a million opportunities to take a shortcut. And that shortcut can look so appealing…that first car you buy that you can't really afford so it owns you instead of you owning it. Nice way to go into bankruptcy before you really get started. Buying that house that you really can't afford so the stress of the debt causes your marriage to unravel. The real trick to getting ahead in life is realizing that things take time. I know that sounds boring, and I'm sorry to have to tell you this, but it takes time to build a life. You've got to be patient because things do pay off eventually.

Television makes it hard to set realistic expectations for ourselves and for our children. Everyone gets everything they want in one episode. Everyone stands around talking most of the time. When do they work, these people on TV? And our kids are watching this. They think that's what life is going to be. And it's important that we tell them that life is work. Sorry for the spoiler, but our kids shouldn't think life is going to be easier than it is. We set them up for failure by insulating them from reality over and over again. Basically, we are financially breastfeeding them until they are finally at an age where they think life is going to be easy, and that's when they crash and burn and move back into our house. So if you want to be fair with kids and really help them, teach them that life is work, and it takes time. There are no shortcuts.

Talent Show

When I was in 8th grade in New Oxford, Pennsylvania, I got my first guitar. I had begged for one for years because I wanted a guitar so much. Kids from families as poor as ours didn't get the things they wanted, but Dad found a guitar at a yard sale for $1, with no strings attached—literally, there were no strings attached. So I spent the next few months playing air guitar and dreaming about what I would do if I ever had real strings that made real music.

My yard sale instrument was an F cut Kay guitar. If you Google F cut Kay guitar, circa 1940-45, you'll find the model. It's the dreadnought of the guitar world with F cuts. It looks like a giant violin. It had the worst action, probably a half an inch, which is a lot of distance to depress the strings down to the fret board to form a chord or a note. I think it was probably the most painful guitar a kid could ever play, but I didn't care. I was so happy to have one at last.

I started teaching myself to play, or at least I tried. My dad played guitar very well, and he did try to teach me once, but he wasn't very patient. He played a song really fast and said to me, "Now you do it." I said, "Dad I have no idea how to do that." He said, "Fine, teach yourself. That's what I did." That was the first and last guitar lesson I ever got from Dad. So I just started trying different things, just hitting strings.

Eventually I composed one little song, and I thought it was pretty good. I was so proud of myself that I entered a talent show at my school in New Oxford. There were about 1700 kids in the audience watching the various performers. I walked onto the stage with my ugly guitar to play my song, but it wasn't really a whole song. It was just one little piece that I played over and over again. The kids started booing because the "song" didn't really go anywhere. I left the stage in disgrace and got on the bus with my big old ugly viola, stand-up, bass-looking guitar. I hated my guitar. I hated my life.

That humiliating experience might have discouraged some kids from continuing to play, but I couldn't quit. I just knew I was supposed to play the guitar. Since I couldn't stop, I had to find people who could help me. One time my teacher was the crazy guy who lived in the trailer next door who played old blues and honky-tonk. I would do chores for him in exchange for the lessons he would give me. I was willing to learn from everyone who had any expertise with the guitar. By taking advantage of every opportunity, a little bit here and a little bit there, I eventually learned to play.

The important lesson I learned from this experience is pretty obvious. You can stay by yourself and hope you can build everything out of your own thinking, or you can associate with other people who can help you. Through my whole life, I collected little pieces of knowledge from the various people I met so I could get better at whatever I wanted to learn. Some of these mentors taught me specific skills, and others added value to my thinking. When I was growing up, it might take weeks or months to find someone to help me. Today there's no barrier between you and all the people who can teach you. Today that learning is ubiquitous. If you look at the millions of videos on YouTube, what is out there that you can't learn? The only one who can stop you is you. I tell kids, "If you want to get good at something, go learn it. Nothing is stopping you. There's a whole world of learning out there." No more excuses, go out there and find the thing you want to learn and then share your talent.

Lights Out

Sometime around 1978 we moved to Decherd, Tennessee. I loved living in Tennessee, and I still love to go back there. I like the way people are there. I always felt like I could be myself in Tennessee. We moved into a trailer park on the outskirts of Decherd. The circumstances of the move were just like they always were: we had just enough money for rent in the trailer park, which meant no money for any utilities, but we were happy to have a house. Poor people figure out how to supply the basics and then worry about how to survive day to day without the amenities others consider essential, like heat and electricity. So Mom, Dad, and five kids moved into the trailer, and we sat in the dark at night with only a couple of oil lamps to dimly light the room while we stared at a television we couldn't turn on. Except for the physical presence of the television, it might as well have been 1878, not 1978.

One night Dad decided he would take a shortcut to get us electricity because that's what Dad always did. He decided he would take a look at the electric pole to see what he could do. It's probably not necessary to give a little background on how electricity is supposed to be activated. Everyone knows when you don't have outstanding late charges on your utilities, the electric company comes out, removes the glass covering, installs a meter, replaces the glass covering, and you have electricity. They also put a lock on the meter that says, "Do not remove under penalty of law" or something like that. So Dad cut the lock off and removed the glass covering because he couldn't meet that "no outstanding late charges" requirement.

I'm sure Dad thought this would be a simple procedure because in his construction work he often roughed in the electrical wiring, and then he would turn on the electricity long enough for them to test their work. To do that, he would take a thick copper wire and bridge the gap between the two contact points, a tried and true technique he'd used many times. However, this particular meter had three contact points, and he'd never seen one like it. I watched him puzzle over this for a few moments as he turned the wire several different directions before finally choosing one direction and jamming the wire into the gap. What happened next defies explanation. The meter didn't just explode; it went molten metal. A sun flare erupted in our faces blinding both of us for over an hour. It wasn't surprising that we destroyed the meter on this pole, but we also blew up the transformer for the entire trailer park.

Dad dropped to the ground and yelled, "Find the wire! Find the wire!" The wire was evidence that we had to hide because as ludicrous as it sounds, we could always claim that somebody drove by and randomly blew up our utility pole. We were back in the trailer sitting quietly in the absolute darkness of the living room, looking like the perfect family unit when the police and the landlord knocked on our door.

"Hey, what's going on?" the landlord inquired.

"Nothing, we're just sitting around," Dad replied.

"Anything weird happen tonight?"

"No, we're just sitting around talking,"

And they didn't arrest Dad. Nothing at all happened, but the consequences could have been much more severe than waiting an hour for our vision to return.

The lesson from this experience is the same as the one from Woodbine. There are no shortcuts. Operating outside of the law, outside of reason, outside of planning like my dad always did never works. When I talk to kids, I always ask them what their plan is to get them from where they are to where they want to be. I remind them that it's a long, difficult, sometimes excruciating process, and if you stand with people who are always looking for shortcuts, you can get blinded by their light just like I did.

Trick or Treat

There was a time growing up when my siblings and I were about 4, 5, and 6 that Dad told us we were going trick-or-treating. We were so excited about the chance to collect candy that it didn't occur to us immediately that it wasn't Halloween. In fact it was summertime, and we didn't have costumes. As we watched Dad drive away in the pickup, we quickly realized this wasn't a normal Halloween outing. He was dumping us. We started chasing the truck screaming, "Dad, Dad, Dad." Fortunately, he saw us running after him and reluctantly stopped the vehicle.

He cursed at us as we clambered in, and I truly believe this was his attempt to get rid of us. He still had an adorable baby at home, and life would be much easier if he could get rid of the three children who required a lot more food, clothing, and attention. I can't begin to know exactly what was in his mind, but I imagine he picked an affluent neighborhood where he thought someone might be moved to take in three waifs as easily as they would adopt a stray cat or dog. Whatever his motive or thought process was, we returned home, but I had picked up some very heavy baggage that day—the thought that I wasn't wanted.

As painful as this experience was, it taught me a valuable lesson that I try to remember whenever I deal with kids who are driving me crazy. I always try to imagine what might be going on in their life, and I show an extra measure of patience. I also try to imagine how I might be a surrogate role model for them. As imperfect as I am, I try to show kids what normal might look like because I'm probably more normal than the chaos that many of them experience at home. To do that, I have to let them in. I have to let students know me beyond my professional persona.

I also have to do an emotional triage on students because we can't treat them all the same. That's not what they need. Just like doctors in an emergency room assess the level of injury, we have to do that with the young people in our lives. Some need a psychic Band-aid, and some have an emotional compound fracture, and it would be grossly unfair to treat them the same way, but that's how we've been trained. Teachers should be fair and equitable with everyone, right? We're so fair that it's unfair how fair we are. Rather than focusing on being fair, focus on giving everyone exactly what he or she needs, and always let students see you as a person. Let them get to know the real you, not just your job title.

Eat and Run

Dad had a scam that he would use when we went out to eat, and it terrified Mom. We would eat a normal meal like everything was fine, and at the end of the meal he would lean in and say softly to everyone, "We're going to eat and run." Dad did this often enough that no further explanation was required. He did this often enough that my stomach hurt whenever we went out to a restaurant because I never knew whether or not we were going to pay for the meal or run as fast as we could out of different doors at the same time so they wouldn't know who to chase.

We were pretty good at the "eat and run" because we executed it many times, and no one ever got caught, but I hated it! I hated it because I knew we could never go to that restaurant again. We had just burned another one off our list, but more importantly, the "eat and run" was wrong. I knew we were being dishonest when we skipped out without paying our bill.

I often tried to figure out what was going through my dad's mind when he made this kind of choice because he wasn't crazy. He grew up in poverty. He was an alcoholic. He was many things, but he wasn't stupid. In fact he was pretty smart in many ways so I'm not sure how he became such a societal parasite.

Rather than understanding and following the rules of society that most people built lives on, he went around the rules at every opportunity. He found a way around the rules that he wouldn't have gotten away with today. His bounced checks would have caught up with him quickly with electronic banking, but you could get away with a lot more back then. Dad would not have liked living in these times.

Even though it was dishonest and terrifying for the family, Dad was trying to do a good thing. He wanted to give his family a nice evening out, and it was sweet that he wanted to do that. However, if he really wanted to do something good for the family, he should have thought about it three weeks in advance and saved the money to pay for the meal. He wanted to **feel** like a nice guy without **being** the nice guy that it really took to get those resources together. As a father, I can empathize with his desire to do something special for his family, but the reality of the "eat and run" was that he ended up punishing us instead.

If you really want to build a life you are proud of, a life where your kids can have new shoes, a life where you can provide special things for your spouse, you have to work hard now. You have to put money in the bank for that, and I don't mean just cash. I mean working on yourself so you are able to make the money you need to give people the life they deserve. Now you might think money's not important, but money is important. I'm sorry about that, but it is. It's not the MOST important thing, and it's not the solution to everything, but the stress caused by a lack of money will ruin your life. It will ruin your marriage. The arguments you have over $10 and $20 take their toll over time.

If you can work hard and build a life free from poverty, your stomach stops hurting and your mind can work on other things. Poverty is very expensive for the mind because the mind worries about your poverty and what you are going to do next. You worry about daily bills, and you worry about sending your kids to college. That drama, while compelling and actually addictive, is not the way to live your life.

I think there are people in the Honeycutt clan who are actually addicted to the drama. They get so used to the drama that they don't know how to live a quiet life where nothing big happens, and the police don't come to the house. At some subconscious level, they almost need the whole thing to come apart because that's what we're good at, putting it back together after it all falls down.

That's what people who don't live in poverty don't understand about the poor. Why do they constantly sabotage themselves? Why do they tear everything down? Why do they burn down their own lives? I think it's because they are more comfortable in chaos than they are in normalcy. As a teacher, I wonder if I can create some element of chaos that's not negative that students can like? Can I create a placeholder for them so they don't burn down their actual life? They will burn it down on a whim, and it will blow your mind if you've never seen this. So work hard, save your money, and help others along the way to build the life you all deserve because nobody should ever have to eat and run!

Shopping for Shoes

As I've said many times, Mom was the glue that held our family together, and she made sure as many of our needs were met as possible. However, Dad was the one who usually took us out shopping for shoes. If you're having a hard time picturing my dad frequenting a Thom McAn store, Famous Footwear, or even Payless ShoeSource with his five kids in tow, you are right to be skeptical because his favorite place to find shoes was the skating rink. It's kind of ingenious when you think about it. Kids take off their shoes for several hours so you have plenty of time to survey the selection and find the perfect size and style. You just leave your old shoes in the slot, and walk away. It was certainly less stressful than the "eat and run."

This is just one example of the crazy things that happen to families in poverty that most people don't know about. People don't understand that kids are taught to do these things. Just like any animal teaches its offspring how to survive, parents in poverty teach their kids how to survive any way they can. Anyone trying to teach these children a better way must remember that their efforts are being undone at home. If you are going to break that cycle of poverty, you need to work with more than the children. You have to work with parents, too. How do you help parents feel a sense of pride that they actually bought shoes for their children, even if they are cheap, vinyl shoes that cost $7.99 and will only last a short time? How do you get kids to work hard for something when they've done it the easy way their entire life?

This is a hard concept for some people to understand. They just get mad and blame the kids, or they blame the family. They don't understand that generational poverty involves indoctrination over many years. This is what we're up against. Please don't think it's impossible. I've seen it turn around. I've seen a teacher work with one student where he or she builds a relationship and shows the child all the possibilities that are out there.

Part of that change process requires an understanding that a successful life requires dedication, a strong work ethic and the determination to stay with something longer than one day or one week. In poverty we think about one week or sometimes one day at a time. If Dad can find some money, we'll eat tonight. We'll eat all of it and be hungry tomorrow. And then the next drama unfolds where we'll try to find money again. That's just the way life works.

I want to help people in these situations, and to help them, I need to show them how to see life bigger, not one day at a time but years at a time. That's the unfair advantage that people with wealth have. They see a big picture. They know how it's going to play out over five years, and they plan carefully. They don't eat everything every day. They parse things out. That's financial literacy. That's not easy, and it's more than balancing a checkbook.

Helping people understand how to manage money is a daunting task. If you want to give someone living in poverty a gift, financial literacy is the best gift you can give. This is why I like to work with kids to build their own businesses so they start seeing how money works, how selling works, how marketing works. They learn first-hand how long it takes to build up cash reserves and how stupid it is to spend it all at one time. They learn how to be careful with money so it sticks to them, as my friend, Deb, is fond of saying. How do you get money to stick to you so you're not always broke, always starting anew every single day? Once you learn that important lesson, your days of shopping for shoes at the skating rink will end.

Rest Area

My earliest childhood memories are of Mom and Dad fighting about money. When I say earliest memories, I'm guessing I was about 3, so my little sister would have been 2 and my older brother about 4½. Dad was usually drunk, and Mom would be angry that Dad's poor choices had burned through what little money we had. At some point in the argument, Dad would have enough of it, and that's when he would put the three of us in the car, and off we would go with him drunk behind the wheel. He did this to punish Mom because he knew she would be scared and worried about us until we got back home. That happened frequently.

On one particular occasion, I don't know how far Dad drove or how long the trip took, but I remember we were all scared. Even though we were very young, we knew what he was doing was dangerous. He was crossing the centerline on the highway, and the speedometer kept creeping up. We were all relieved when Dad finally pulled into a rest area and passed out on the ground next to the car. Not knowing what else to do, we got out of the car and played in the rest area all night in the blue-green glow of the mercury-vapor lights. We were totally at the mercy of the universe while Dad slept it off, but we were undoubtedly safer there than in the car with him behind the wheel. Today I reflect on that experience with a bit of amazement, and perhaps that explains my fascination with rest areas. I talk about them frequently because in a way, they feel like home. That night it was an oasis of light that made us feel safe. Everyone had a place in the light away from the darkness. We didn't have to be rich. All we had to do was show up, and we had access to everything the rest area had to offer. The idea that rest areas were places where families came to have picnics also intrigued me because that's not how it worked in my family, but I wanted that for myself, and I wanted it for my kids when I became an adult.

When I left home, I was determined to have the normal life I dreamed of as a child. One thing I learned from my parents' endless fighting was that your relationship with your spouse determines the kind of life you build to an enormous degree. How you interact and treat one another means everything. It seems pretty obvious to say that a marriage filled with love and mutual respect will be happier than one filled with animosity, but it's not always as obvious that your kids are looking at that relationship to learn how to treat a spouse. They are learning what love is, what parenting is, and they are learning all of that from you. So the foundation of building a great life comes from the person you choose to marry. We have to teach our children that this is one of the most, if not THE most, important decisions they will make in their lives. We have to teach our children that even if they find the perfect person, marriage will still take a lot of work. A successful marriage takes commitment. It takes two people saying, "We are not going to stop. No matter what, we won't stop. We'll work together until we figure this out." That's what couples need to strive for as they build a life together.

Growing up without strong role models to show me this example was hard. Here's the thing you have to know when someone goes through life like that; it doesn't just go away. Don't you wish you could just wash it off and it would be gone? It's dangerous to think you can do that because it will come back to bite you in your weak moments so you have to constantly be vigilant to avoid the habits and behavior patterns that are seared into your psyche. You have to embrace what's been done to you. You have to intentionally turn it into something good.

And that's what I'm trying to do by sharing my story. I want to take these crazy things and turn them into some lessons that someone can use because I don't want all of that pain to be wasted. I thank God that I found my wife and somehow she chose to stay with me through the good and the bad. We shared the same commitment to our relationship so we persevered. With her help, I am becoming the man I was meant to be. Developing that special relationship has been the key to building my own personal Rest Area.

Foster Home

My memory is a little fuzzy on the exact date, but I believe I was four because I wasn't in school yet so my sister would have been three and my brother would have been in kindergarten or first grade the time we went to live with my grandparents. My mom and dad dropped us by our grandparents' house in Ottawa, Kansas at these tender ages so they could look for work. It's a little surprising that Grandma and Grandpa agreed to watch us for an extended period of time because they went out to the tavern every night and drank, and that was basically their lifestyle.

Grandpa had served in World War II, and there were a lot of things I admired about him, but when he drank, he was a maniacal person who did some pretty terrible things. Grandma wasn't much better when they were drinking, but when you live a life of poverty and chaos, all the elements of your family are in play. Leaving your kids with their alcoholic grandparents might seem to be your only choice, but you know you do that with some risk. My parents felt they had to take that risk because Mom couldn't care for us and look for work so they dropped us off for what was to be a short stay. Mom and Dad had no idea at the time that it would be many months before we were reunited as a family.

I'm not sure how long we were actually there, but it didn't take us long to learn that the rules in my grandparents' house were very different from the rules in our house. Children were to be seen and not heard, which meant you couldn't talk or touch anything. Grandma had ten million little trinkets she called whatnots. These included salt and pepper shakers from every state, plus a million other little tchotchkes that we weren't allowed to touch. We were in perpetual trouble for touching these things that were so amazing that you just couldn't help yourself. Eventually my grandparents must have had their fill of us talking and touching things, or they decided that we had been dumped on them permanently, and they took us down to the SRS office where they declared that we had been abandoned. Things moved pretty quickly at this point, and we were placed in a foster home.

As a child of poverty, I had plenty of experience with state institutions, and whenever I brushed up against them, they were always the same: they smelled like Pine Sol, and they felt serious and formal. Schools were in that category. Schools smelled and felt like SRS. They were all institutions made out of cinder block, and you know it was the rare school that actually felt like home. I rarely found a classroom that felt like a warm, inviting place to be. Institutions can be intimidating for many people, but for a kid who comes from poverty, institutions are scary. Most of the time the institution is foreign to the child, and often the services feel like something that is unnecessary and unwanted. Putting a child in an institution is like bringing a wild animal into a house and expecting them to be normal. So we brought a little of the wild with us when we went to the foster home.

The foster home we stayed at was in eastern Kansas, and the family members were Dunkards. I don't know if they were German Baptist Dunkards, but they were the people that wear the black skirts and the black outfits and the caps on their heads. The "Dad" had a beard and a hat, and the house had no radio or TV. To be fair, we would have been in shock wherever we went, but it was quite a cultural awakening to move into this house with these people who seemed very odd to us. When we arrived, they sat us on the couch to tell us the rules. As "Dad" was explaining things, it became apparent that my three-year-old sister had pooped her pants. He asked if she had soiled herself. I don't think she understood the word "soiled", but he was also very scary and intimidating so she shook her head "No". And then for lying to him he slapped her in the mouth with his open hand and split both of her lips right there in front of my brother and me. At the age of four, one thought went through my mind, "I will kill this man. When I am grown, I will kill this man." To have that thought as a four year old indicates how deeply that incident affected me.

We were in that foster home for months while my parents worked to get us out. Mom and Dad had to prove they had jobs and a house. It took a very long time to navigate the bureaucratic process, but we eventually got out of that place. We were so happy to be picked up by our dysfunctional family because as bad as things were with Dad, it was better than what we had experienced in the foster home. That seems to fly in the face of conventional wisdom because the foster home had more structure and higher expectations, more rigor if you will, but to us everything about it was punitive. No one there tried to see things from our perspective or understand our background.

So the lesson from this experience is that you can't change lives with tough rules and intimidation. That doesn't mean that you have to coddle people or eliminate consequences for bad behavior. That does mean you can take everyone toward a better set of expectations. You simply have to meet everyone where they are and bring them along. I know achieving that goal isn't as simple as it sounds, but humans are complicated beings, and when damage is done to them, it takes a long time to overcome the trauma. If we don't take the time and effort to help them heal, they can turn their life experience into an excuse for why their life didn't work. It takes patience and a very special person to help others overcome their individual "foster home" experience, but it's well worth the effort.

Taking Things Slowly

Growing up in poverty meant that we seldom had nice things so we were understandably excited on those rare occasions when something beautiful or valuable came into our lives. That's exactly what happened one day when we were living in an old farmhouse near Brushtown, Pennsylvania, and Dad arrived home with a collie. I have no idea where he got this dog, but she was beautiful, especially compared to the stray animals, both wild and domestic, that were our usual pets. As he tied her to a tree, Dad cautioned us saying, "Now, she's been abused, and she's really scared, so you have to come up to her really, really, slowly…gently now."

In our excitement, we surrounded the dog like curious villagers and squealed with delight at our good fortune. "She is such a cute dog!" "She's so beautiful!" The collie responded with a look of absolute terror in her eyes. Not picking up on the dog's obvious physical cues, Dad released the collar from the rope, and she disappeared like a puff of smoke. We watched her kick up clouds of dust across the freshly plowed fields around the farm. We watched her become smaller and smaller as she covered the two mile distance to the nearby woods. We continued to stare at the dust hanging in the air like a low-level contrail. The whole family just stood there in absolute silence as we marveled at the amazing velocity the dog achieved before she disappeared into the tree line. We looked for the dog in the woods with flashlights and continued the search for several days, but we all knew that we no longer had a dog.

I learned a valuable lesson the day the dog ran away. Whether you are dealing with an animal or a person who has been abused in any way, you have to wait to be invited into their space. You have to move at their speed. You can't rush in and expect to be trusted. You sit with them. You honor them. You wait until they feel comfortable. It can be frustrating at times, but the only way to establish a long-term relationship and make a difference is to take things slowly.

Free Lunch

My entire family went through a very difficult time right after my sister was injured in an explosion in Woodbine, Maryland. The gas leak that put her in the hospital left us homeless until we moved into a slum apartment in New Windsor, Maryland. Even though the rent was free because of the accident and truckloads of donated clothing came flooding in, we were in bad shape. Most of the clothing should have been thrown away, but it was all we had so that was what we wore to school.

Mom was going to Baltimore to the burn unit to be with my sister every day, and the rest of us were just surviving with Dad. Dad must have been living on alcohol alone because the only thing in the refrigerator for weeks at a time was a jar of mayonnaise. Dad seemed to have plenty of money for beer, somehow, but none for food. So the one thing we had to look forward to was eating a free meal at school.

When we enrolled, we got our free lunch tickets, and I recognized right away that mine was a different color than the other tickets. I was horrified to think that everyone in line would know I was eating a free lunch because of the color of my ticket. And I couldn't do that. So I just didn't eat. The whole time I went to school there I just drank water at lunch so my stomach wouldn't hurt. Then I went home to a house with no food in it all because of the color of my lunch ticket.

It might be difficult to understand the mentality of people in poverty, but I still had my pride. I know it's crazy, right? How can you afford pride when you are hungry? Well, you do because sometimes your pride is the only thing you have. You are already embarrassed because you know you are poor, and you don't want to go to school and try to fit into a culture with the liability of everyone else knowing that you are poor, too. Even though your clothes are showing it, and your hair is showing it, and every other thing about you is screaming it, you don't need more social liabilities, you just don't.

I've thought about my experience with a free lunch ticket, and even if technology has eliminated that particular stigma, the way we treat kids at school hasn't changed much over the years. We still give them inadvertent liabilities that hinder their ability to fit in and be successful. School culture can be mean, and kids will develop a *Lord of the Flies* mentality if we let them. We create an artificial society that students are mandated to join, and often the people in charge don't have any control over what happens there. The teachers and the administrators play a big role in the school life of a child, and they have to serve as role models for kids who don't have them at home. Educators are responsible for the things that happen to every student, every day. Whether we acknowledge it or not, the custodial care provided by schools is just as important, if not more so, than the educational experience. I don't think any kid should come home feeling worse than they did when they left the house.

The schools that are able to solve this problem are the ones that spend more than two days a year building a positive culture. They proactively work on it every day. They engage kids in the process. They make sure that everyone understands that the way a student **feels** during learning is more important than any specific concept or skill he or she masters. They provide the trained staff necessary to deal with the issues that destroy a healthy culture like poverty, abuse, neglect, and intolerance. When all of those things are in place, the color of students' lunch tickets won't matter because they will know they are safe, supported, and free from judgment.

Staying with Grandpa and Grandma

Grandma and Grandpa Sullivan were my dad's mother and stepdad, and they lived a very meager life. I don't mean that in a disparaging way, but they were living on Social Security so they didn't have much. Since both of them were diabetic and poor, the kitchen cabinet was pretty sparse. They couldn't have sugar, and there was very little in the way of sugar substitutes back then, except for saccharin. The entertainment at their house matched the cuisine as they had a little black and white TV with a 12-inch screen, and that was it. Welcome to Grandpa and Grandma's house.

None of us ever wanted to go to their house, much less stay, because there was never anything to do. However, to assuage his guilt for never visiting his mom, dad would occasionally leave one of us for an extended stay. That was his gift to her, an indentured servant for a week. I had no problem helping out with the chores at Grandpa and Grandma's house, but it was a hard life, even by Honeycutt standards, and the entertainment options were almost non-existent. Imagine if you can, sitting around at night watching their tiny black and white TV while my visually impaired grandparents made their best guess as to what was happening on the show. It was obvious by their narrative that they weren't following the plot so I would try to help when Grandma would say things like, "She's gonna keell him."

"No Grandma, she loves him; they are going to get married."

"No, she's gonna keell him dead." It didn't take many exchanges like that before I would just quit arguing and let them watch the show they thought they were watching while I viewed something entirely different.

Bright and early every morning I had chores to do, and mowing the grass was my main job. It wouldn't have been such a monumental task if they'd had anything other than an old, rotary style lawn mower. The lack of a motor would have been challenging enough, but it was always rusted solid in between visits so I would have to oil it every time and try my best to sharpen the blade with a rock because Grandpa never had any tools. Despite all my effort, the mower would mostly slide through the grass with an occasional turn of the blades so it took forever to mow their lawn. Even as an eighth grader pushing this antique through the grass in Glenelg, Maryland in 1979, I knew my job was much harder than it should have been. I also knew that after I was done, Grandpa would insist on paying me because he was a man who believed an honest day's work deserved an honest day's pay. So he would give me a quarter. A quarter! I couldn't believe he thought an entire day's work was worth a quarter! I felt like I was in a bad Depression Era movie.

Taking my "pay" across the street to the only store around was always an adventure. The elderly lady who worked and lived in the building sold candy that could only be found in her store because it had been out of production for many years. Even if you didn't know that fact, the layer of dust covering everything was a great clue. So I would buy some horehound candy or whatever other confectionary relic was on the shelf along with one chocolate football. That's what I could afford on my coolie wages, one chocolate football and four pieces of horehound candy.

When I would get back home, my grandfather would say, "Bring it over here!" The first time it happened, I couldn't believe that Grandpa looked over my purchase and took the only decent piece for himself. He cherry-picked my freaking candy football, my chocolate football. How could my diabetic grandfather take my only good piece of candy I had just worked a whole day to earn and leave me with four pieces of horehound candy that were basically inedible? I mean Laura Ingalls Wilder did not have choices, but this was 1979.

As I said before, the culinary choices at my grandparent's house were minimal, and often what was available was hard to believe. One day at breakfast I noticed that my milk had something floating in it so I said, "Grandma there's something in my milk." To this she replied, "Oh, don't worry about it. When grandpa finishes his cereal, he pours his milk back in the jug." So the floaters I saw were the cereal remnants from his previous (who knew exactly how many) bowls of cereal. My reaction can only be described as a total freak out, but Grandma made it clear that no one was allowed to waste anything. She said, "You will sit there until you drink that milk." So I sat there for a good three hours until they both left the room, and I poured the milk on a houseplant that I'm pretty sure recoiled in horror at the indignity.

To supplement the groceries, Grandma picked her own food in the wild because she'd grown up in West Virginia and Tennessee, and she knew what you could eat, or at least she used to know when she was able to see. Now she foraged and cooked by Braille, rather than by sight, and she would pick the leaves off of things she called wild greens. Poke was one of her favorites, and as she pulled off these broad leaves she would say, "Kevin, I want you to look close here because if you accidentally eat that purple part it will keell you dead. It's poison; that purple part's poison." As she was tearing it along the purple and green line, I was silently admonishing her, "Please tear carefully. I don't want to die at your house tonight!" After the leaves were torn apart, she would start boiling the poke, and it smelled like grass clippings. It would boil all day long just to get it tender and then that night it was like "WOO HOO! We get to eat grass clippings and recycled milk." So I had the whole day to dread supper, but that's what we had so that's what we ate.

Occasionally, they would go to the Food Rite store, and Grandpa always drove. If Grandma cooked using Braille, Grandpa DROVE using Braille. It was pretty obvious he couldn't see; the man was all over the road. I prayed to God the entire trip, and I can truthfully say I've never been closer to Jesus in my life than I was during those drives with Grandpa at the wheel.

There's a thing I called being current with the Lord. That means, right now, if I die, I'm going to heaven because I have asked for forgiveness. So if you think any nasty thoughts after you say that, you have to re-pray again and ask for forgiveness again. All the way to the store I would make sure I was current with the Lord because I knew Grandpa was going to crash any minute. Grandma was no help because she couldn't see either so she didn't know how close we were to hitting things like bridges. Unfortunately my vision was perfect so I would be in the back seat saying, "Grandpa, watch out for the bridge!"

"What bridge?"

"The bridge over the river! You are about to hit the bridge!" It was like that all the way to the store. Once we stopped, all I could do was kiss the ground and thank God I was still alive, and then we'd go in the store.

The first time I went to the grocery store with my grandparents, I was appalled to see Grandma head to the produce section where she started eating all the fruit she wanted. She'd eat strawberries and grapes, not to check the quality, just to gorge on anything that looked good.

"Grandma! That's illegal! You're shop-lifting! They're going to put you in jail!"

"They're not going to put an old woman in jail."

To avoid any guilt by association, I went over to see Grandpa who was negotiating a deal at the meat counter. This was where his speech impediment became a big problem. He was trying to buy roast beef, but he called it Roaf Meef. I understood him because I was around him all the time, but the young guy behind the meat counter wasn't as successful. Grandpa would say, "I want five pounds of Roaf Meef."

"What?"

"Roaf Meef," Grandpa repeated.

"Excuse me?"

"Roaf Meef! Roaf Meef!" Grandpa was screaming in anger at this point, and Grandma was still stealing fruit so there was no safe place in the store for me. I just wandered around the aisles hoping to God that this would end soon. When we finally got to the checkout line, I saw that Grandma did not buy any fruits or vegetables, so none of that was going home with us. It was back to cereal milk and wild greens.

As we waited in line, Grandma did what Grandma was well known for—she passed gas, loudly. Whenever she felt the need, that's what happened, and more often than not, it sounded like someone tuning a trombone. Without missing a beat, she turned around and said, "Kevin! I'm surprised at you!" As if I hadn't suffered enough indignities already associating with a shoplifter and Roaf Meef Man, my own grandmother tried to hang her fart on me! "Grandma, you know it was you!" Everyone in the line, of course, turned to look at me like I'm the worst grandson in the world, having just done this terrible thing and blaming my grandma for it. Grandpa and Grandma were laughing and cackling about the joke on me as we got in the car and took the death ride home.

At long last, Dad would show up at the end of the week after you had survived all these things. I loved my family, but I never loved them more than I did when they came to pick me up from Grandpa and Grandma's house. You not only felt differently, you acted differently when they picked you up. "Mother, father, sisters, brothers. I love thee!" Arguments with the siblings disappeared because I was so grateful to be back. As bad as my house could be, I was used to that kind of bad.

I know I learned something from that particular experience, but I'm not sure how to label it. Maybe I learned tolerance. Even though living their life was difficult for me, I learned not to judge them too harshly just because their daily existence was different from mine. Maybe the lesson I learned was to stop before you put down someone else's life, and try it on to see what you can learn from it. Maybe the lesson was to appreciate what you have because someone out there is always worse off than you. I'm still trying to make sense of what I learned from those times, but one thing I know for sure is that I will never forget staying with Grandpa and Grandma.

Bubble Yum Tycoon

I became an accidental entrepreneur when I was in the seventh grade. Money was scarce so I was always looking for any opportunity to earn extra cash to spend on the finer things in life like bubble gum. I never dreamed that my love for that lowly confection would turn me into the Bubble Yum Tycoon of New Windsor, Maryland.

I bought a pack of Bubble Yum, which I think still comes with five pieces in a pack. I took my Bubble Yum to school, and suddenly kids wanted to buy pieces from me. I chewed one piece, and sold the rest for enough money that I was able to buy two packs of Bubble Yum later that day. I started doing that every day until I had an extensive inventory of gum in my locker.

I expanded my business to include Tasty Cakes. If you live in or near Pennsylvania, you know about the peanut buttery slice of heaven that is a Tasty Cake. Those things are delicious and paired with the Bubble Yum, I was selling merchandise like crazy from my tiny store and learning many important lessons about running a business. I had to determine a price for my products that made a reasonable profit without being too expensive for my customers. Additionally, I had to keep enough inventory on hand to meet the demand and complete my transactions without making anyone late for class. I was making really good money until the school found out and shut me down. I don't think I was violating any commerce laws, but my days as a chewing gum magnate ended abruptly.

Schools today are encouraging students to start businesses and develop their entrepreneurial skills. Those are important lessons to learn because you will always be selling something as an adult whether you are selling yourself to a prospective employer or a product that you believe in, even if it's just bubble gum.

Earthworm Opportunity

Reselling Bubble Yum and Tasty Cakes might have been my first business venture, but it certainly wasn't my last. After Dad died, life in our trailer in Pomona, Kansas was pretty rough. Mom was the janitress at the schools, but we had a hard time paying all the bills. We would get behind on the rent often, and then Mom would have to ask the grocery store to extend the line of credit. It was a hard existence so any additional opportunity to earn money that came our way was a blessing.

One of those opportunities came on the heels of a warm, steady rain that fell for about three or four days. Towards the end of this continual precipitation, I found myself having trouble sleeping one night so I went outside to look around. I saw something moving in the mud and bent down to pick up a nightcrawler off the ground. As I looked around, I spotted another one, and another one, and another one. Everywhere I looked there were night-crawlers. They must have been coming out of the ground because of the saturation.

Living near Pomona Lake, I had purchased nightcrawlers at the bait shop many times so I knew the ground was covered with slimy, slithering nickels. Without much thought, I just started picking them up. I spent the whole night filling this huge tub with nightcrawlers, thousands and thousands of these things. It was the most amazing night. When I was finished, I felt like I had a pot of gold. I knew that nightcrawlers liked to eat coffee grounds so I mixed some in with the dirt. By carefully tending the earthworms, I maintained a business that brought me income for several months.

We never had another saturating rain like that while we lived in Pomona, but I learned a valuable lesson from my business. I learned to look for those opportunities that other people miss. You might have an incredible opportunity in front of you right now. Look around for that. I attune myself to that now because I want to be ready when the next gentle rain brings another earthworm opportunity.

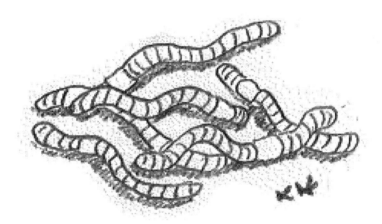

Dad and the Blunderbuss

It's important for kids to help around the house to learn responsibility. One of my jobs growing up was to hide the guns when Dad was drinking. I know he shot at least one person, and possibly more, so there was never any doubt that he was a dangerous man. I had a secret place under the house where I would hide the guns, and he would get very, very angry when he couldn't find them. Of course I never bothered to hide the blunderbuss he had hanging on the wall because it wasn't a dangerous firearm. I don't know what Pilgrim ancestor Dad got the thing from, but it was definitely an antique that hadn't been fired in decades, perhaps centuries.

Dad sold used cars for a period of time, and they were all junkers that didn't belong on the road. He could do things to get them to run for a while, but sooner or later the car's real condition would become apparent. That's the kind of stuff my dad did, and sometimes his customers would refuse to pay for the lemons he sold them. In response to the non-payment, Dad often would get liquored up and decide he was going to shoot the deadbeat. That's how my drunken dad ended up in Texarkana, Texas with my drunken Uncle Larry and his blunderbuss.

Dad and Uncle Larry drove to the house of a man who owed money on a car he purchased, and as they got out of their car, shots rang out. PEW! PEW! PEW! Bullets went singing by their heads. They both took cover initially, but Dad was able to sneak up to the house and tap on the window. When the man looked out the window, Dad raised the blunderbuss and pulled back the hammer. I don't know how dad thought a flintlock was going to function, but before he could pull the ancient trigger he heard, "FREEZE!" and the entire Texarkana police force had him surrounded. Of course the entire town knew about the incident by the next morning, but it turned out that the gun wasn't operable so Dad didn't go to jail. However, the guy shooting at him did get arrested. That's the kind of dumb luck my dad had in many of his dealings. Even though Dad wasn't the best teacher, I learned what I shouldn't do by watching his actions, and I was able to avoid following in his footsteps. I never knew what happened to Dad's blunderbuss. I just knew I wasn't going to need it.

Do the Right Thing

We moved so many times when I was young that I had a hard time making friends, and I was never very popular. We weren't in any one place long enough for anyone to really get to know me. My circumstances changed a little when we lived in Pomona, KS. After my dad died, we stayed in Pomona, and I was able to graduate from high school there. I didn't suddenly become "Mr. Popularity," but I was elected vice-president of student council, and I felt as connected and accepted as I ever had anywhere. Most of my friends, including my best friend, Paul, were the misfits and oddballs of the school. Because I was still something of an outsider as well, I never considered the fact that my modicum of acceptance might be jeopardized one day. If I had to choose between helping a friend and being a part of the mainstream crowd, would I do the right thing?

Paul was the closest thing I had to a life-long friend. We went to Hawthorne Elementary School together the first time I lived in Pomona in the late 1970s. When my family moved back, we picked up our friendship right where we left off. Paul was smart, good-natured and weird. Not crazy, laugh-and-point weird, but just enough different that the rank and file of Pomona High School had little tolerance for his eccentricities. The day he told me he was going to wear his karate gi to weightlifting class, I knew there would be trouble. I tried to talk him out of it, but he wouldn't listen.

As I predicted, when he showed up for class wearing his karate training uniform with a white tunic top and pants, a couple of guys took exception to the outfit. Words were exchanged and tensions escalated until it was determined that a fight at the quarry after school was the only way to settle things. Paul was a pretty big kid so I thought he could handle himself in a fair fight, but I went along as his sole supporter since the entire high school seemed to be rooting against him. Where I'm from, if you can't beat me by yourself, you need to stay at home so I assumed Paul would fight the two guys one at a time to see if either of them could give him the beating he apparently deserved because he was different.

The fight started, and Paul was more than holding his own against the first guy. Suddenly the second guy jumped in and it was two against one. I'll never forget how Paul continued to fight and even land some blows, but the odds were clearly against him. Without hesitation I was in the middle of the melee. I didn't punch anyone, but I grabbed the second guy and told him to stop. All at once the crowd grabbed me. I must have had 50 people pulling, lifting, kicking and punching me until Paul and I were completely separated.

It didn't take the two of them long to finish with Paul, and when the crowd dispersed, we looked at one another lying on the ground, bruised and bloodied. The jeers and taunts from the student body as they drove away actually made us laugh. We both realized that a little physical pain was a small price to pay for the knowledge we gained that day. Paul knew he had a true friend who would always stand beside him, and I never worried again about whether or not I would do the right thing.

Glowing Heater

Shortly after Dad powered down the entire neighborhood trying to steal electricity, Mom got a job cleaning hotel rooms, and she was able to pay our bills. I'm not sure what Dad was doing, but at least we had power legally. However, without a central heating unit, we had to rely on one small space heater to provide warmth. The unit was always in Mom and Dad's bedroom so my siblings and I stayed bundled up in our rooms most of the time. We weren't supposed to go into Mom and Dad's bedroom, but sometimes I would get so cold that I'd sneak in on my hands and knees and nestle between the heater and the bed in my cozy little sanctuary. The red glow of the heating elements and the buzz of the noisy little fan had a hypnotic effect on me. Warmed and mesmerized, I could dream of a different life.

Unfortunately, my reverie usually didn't last long. My brothers and sisters would figure out I was in Mom and Dad's room, and they would try to sneak in as well. Of course it's pretty hard to keep five kids quiet at the foot of a bed so it wouldn't be long before Dad caught on and kicked us out. On those rare occasions when no one found me, I would spend hours by myself looking at the elements of the heater, feeling the benevolence of that warmth coming out, and I would think, "Man this is so nice. Wouldn't it be wonderful if you were warm like this all the time?"

Even as a child, I longed for a different future. My dreams weren't very big at that time. I just wanted a heater in every room that stayed on all the time so nobody was ever cold. Over the years, my dreams got bigger, and I worked hard to make them a reality, but I never forgot that little heater burning brightly in the night, igniting a glowing spark of hope in a desperate little boy.

Having It All

Living in Texas near my Aunt Arlene and Uncle Ronnie meant my dad always had a drinking buddy, but Uncle Ronnie was out-going, kind, and funny when he drank, the complete opposite of Dad. Their drinking got so bad at one point that Mom and Aunt Arlene decided they would move in together, and the men could be left to fend for themselves. Instead of coming to their senses and realizing they had gone too far, the men looked at this as an opportunity to live it up. During this time, I never saw either one of them sober so I would guess they drank all day, every day. I'm sure in their minds they were having it all.

Well, they were having it all until the day Uncle Ronnie started vomiting blood. He was rushed to the hospital and diagnosed with cirrhosis of the liver. He didn't respond to treatment, and he died less than 24 hours later leaving all of us devastated, particularly his wife and children.

I know Dad felt guilty about this, but it didn't change his behavior. However, it created a lasting impression on me. I learned that having it all could be dangerous when the things you want are bad choices. I haven't always made the right choices in my life, but the memory of Uncle Ronnie and Dad has helped me get my life back on course many times.

The Lottery

After our house in Woodbine, Maryland exploded and we moved to the slum apartment in New Windsor, Maryland, things were pretty dire for a number of months, maybe close to a year. We had experienced hard times before, but this was a new level of misery. Mom was at the hospital with my sister in Baltimore for long stretches of time, and the rest of us were home with Dad, who was consumed with guilt because of the explosion and the injury to my sister. Whenever Dad experienced hardship of any kind, he went to the depths of his alcoholism. And when he did that, nothing else happened. Nothing else happened. Groceries didn't get purchased, bills didn't get paid, and kids didn't receive any care.

No one at school knew how desperate we were, but you would think someone would have noticed that I wasn't eating lunch. There was no way I was going to let anyone know I was eating free lunches. So I wasn't eating at school, and at home we had that familiar jar of mayonnaise in the refrigerator. Given our dire circumstances, it's not surprising that I would dream about winning the lottery as a way out of our poverty.

I know many middle class families dream about winning the lottery, but they don't look at that phenomenon in the same way poor people do. We think if God loves us, we will win the lottery. We believe that divine intervention, also known as luck to those without a religious background, is the only chance we have to turn things around. Families in poverty have an external locus of control. Everything in life results from forces outside our control, and resistance is futile as they say.

In the midst of this scarcity and dreams of the lottery, I had some numbers pop into my head one day. I thought about them all day long, and I couldn't shake the feeling that this was a sign so I said, "Mom, I think I know the lottery numbers." Of course she said, "Ah, you're full of crap." Then I told my Dad, "I think I know the lottery numbers!" And he said the same thing followed by the fact that we didn't have a dollar to waste. Undeterred by their lack of support, I wrote my numbers down on a piece of paper, and that night we all sat in front of the television to await the announcement of the numbers. You can probably guess what happened--they called my numbers. It was like the universe was trying to help, and I couldn't take advantage of it. My family stared at my paper in shock for a moment, and then they all erupted with "if only" and "what could have been!"

I often think about that lottery we could have won, and I try to imagine what would have happened to us. My gut tells me that we would have been poor again in a year. I say that because like so many other lottery winners, my family had no financial literacy, and if you don't know how money works, you will continue to make the same mistakes you have always made. However, that experience did teach me to believe in myself and to follow my instincts when I know something is right. It also helped me change my attitude about luck. I mean, if I couldn't win the lottery when I knew the numbers, maybe relying on luck wasn't the answer. That's when I decided the way out of poverty was to make my own luck because life is too precious to leave to chance.

Sandwiches

The Honeycutt clan wasn't overly religious, but we did attend church from time to time. We also weren't overly committed to any religious doctrine so we tried out a variety of denominations, and as long as they had some music and talked about God, we were pretty happy. One church that I particularly liked was in Texarkana, TX. Members of the congregation played guitars and drums during the service, and everyone was warm and friendly. It was such a pity we had to cut our ties with them because of sandwiches.

Our last Sunday in attendance, the pastor announced that the church was sponsoring a sandwich feed after the service, and everyone was invited to attend. Free food was always welcome in our family so the decision to stay for lunch was an easy one to make. The sandwiches were daintily cut on the diagonal, and stacked very neatly on serving trays. The great panache that went into the presentation was lost on my family as we consumed the sandwiches like ravenous animals, eating until we couldn't hold anymore. Only after we finished did we find out that each half sandwich was $1.00, not free as we assumed. I think among the 7 of us we probably ate around 100 of those half sandwiches, but Dad didn't have any money so the exact count was irrelevant. Our course of action was clear. We were going to pull an "eat and run" on the Lighthouse Assembly of God Church. One by one we edged toward the door, made our break, and never went back.

I don't know why Dad didn't simply explain the situation to the person in charge. Isn't the mission of the church to feed the hungry? I think the congregation would have been sympathetic to our situation. That experience taught me the importance of working through my embarrassment or insecurity and facing my problems rather than giving up on something or someone important to me. I really missed the music and fellowship we found with that congregation, and yes, I missed those tasty sandwiches, too.

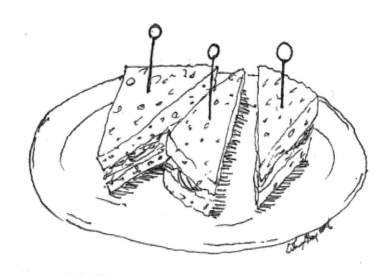

The Meat Deal

I think most of the lessons I've learned in life have a universal application for others even if they didn't grow up in an impoverished, co-dependent household. However, as an educator, I often look closely for classroom connections and how my experience can help teachers. One of those close connections has to be the Meat Deal. If you've been teaching more than a year or two, you've had a student who tried to use it.

Kids growing up in poverty learn how to become grifters. Grifters are amazingly talented people at getting what they want through manipulation. It is very easy to get pulled into their web and become co-dependent with them. They may be lacking in some areas, but what they do know is how to survive because they have had to do that from a very young age. I was still in grade school when dad taught us how to play the "meat deal." We used it most often after moving into a new house because that's when we were usually at our lowest point financially and had no money for food. Dad would go into the store and say, "I bought a roast in here a few days ago, and it was bad." The manager would typically ask, "Do you have a receipt?" Dad would respond, "You mean to tell me when a person buys a roast in this store, he needs to save the receipt?" That would usually work, but he was always prepared to take it to another level, a really loud level if necessary. To avoid a scene in front of other customers, the manager would always say, "We will take care of you. What do you need?" What Dad needed was a five pound roast to feed the family.

It wasn't long before Dad stayed out in the truck and sent me in to play the meat deal. If you are little and cute, you usually don't have to get too loud to make a score. There were other versions of the meat deal. There was the drive through McDonald's deal. It was just like the meat deal except you had to be really loud so that the customers inside the McDonald's could hear you. It was a very unusual skill set, but I learned it well. I was willing to scorch the earth to get what I wanted because that's what Dad needed me to do. I could be loud and embarrassing without a second thought.

I did those things for food, and food can be a powerful motivator when you are hungry, but kids can be motivated by other things that are just as important to their survival. When kids feel disrespected, criticized, or ignored, they can get loud and be inappropriate in ways that are shocking to us. Just remember that self-preservation is a powerful instinct, and the meat deal might just be how they learned to survive.

The Fouke Monster

Most of us experienced nightmares at some point in our childhood. These nightmares can be caused by events ranging from school starting to a death in the family. Given the chaotic circumstances in my life, it's not surprising that I was frequently plagued by nightmares. I think they were worsened by Dad's choice of scary movies whenever we went to the drive in theater. When we moved to Texarkana, Texas, which is just down the road from Fouke, Arkansas, I had one more thing to plague my sleep: the Fouke Monster!

If you're not from anywhere near Fouke, Arkansas, you might not know the legend of the Fouke Monster. The Fouke Monster is the southern version of Bigfoot. There's even a movie called "The Legend of Boggy Creek" where a bunch of unsuspecting teenagers are staying at a house out in the wilderness, and the Fouke Monster attacks. Since we lived near Fouke, I heard about the legend often, and every night I had a nightmare that the Fouke Monster came to my window to get me. Our house out in the woods was just remote enough to be a prime target in my mind.

My brother and I were wrestling in bed one night, and one of us kicked the window and it shattered. Dad was angry and refused to replace the glass or board up the hole. So now, not only was a Fouke Monster roaming the countryside, we had a broken window giving him easy access to the younger brother who slept next to the drafty opening. For weeks I awoke terrified as each nightmare became more intense. Then one night I took control of the situation in what I can only describe as a lucid dream.

I'm not sure exactly how it happened. I was dreaming, yet somehow partially conscious because I had the ability to control the dream. Maybe my subconscious finally took control to rescue me from my fear and frustration. In my lucid dream, I jumped through the window, got in my dad's truck, and started it with my finger because that's how it works in dreams. I chased the Fouke Monster all over the yard in my dad's truck, and that dream went away forever.

That was the beginning of something empowering in my life. I started developing the ability to say, "I'm tired of being afraid of things. I'm going to take control." It didn't happen overnight, but slowly I started to turn my frustration and anger into action. I stopped being a victim and responded to situations in whatever way I could. I believe that we can all do that; we can find that braver person inside us and take control of our Fouke Monsters.

The Legacy of Shame

Bedwetting, much like my nightmares, was caused by the fear and insecurity in my life. The idea of getting out of bed when there were monsters that could grab my feet was something I couldn't overcome. So, I was a chronic bed wetter, and the more it happened, the more frustrated Dad got. He thought he could punish me out of it or reward me out of it. What he never understood was that the solution was in him, not me. If he could have provided a more stable home or if he could have stopped drinking, my fears and my bedwetting would have disappeared. That solution would have taken hard work on his part and a real commitment so he chose a different approach, one that left me with a legacy of shame.

Initially, he would try to bribe me with some prize or treat, which doesn't sound so bad on the surface. But each time I would fail to stay dry, my shame would grow. I'd not only lose the coveted prize, I would see the disappointment and frustration in his eyes. Since he was making such an issue out of my bedwetting, it became fodder for my siblings as well so I had teasing and nicknames at every turn. I think that's why I have such an affinity for the kids who look different and smell different. I know they are barely surviving and navigating a daily roller coaster of emotional realities, and so I try to be a benevolent person who doesn't judge them because I know they will be amazing people some day if we just give them the opportunity.

Shame has a powerful effect on people. I was so ashamed that I would get up every morning, pull off my bed sheet, find a place to hide it, and flip the mattress over. That was my routine every morning. I don't know what happened to that mattress, but I sincerely hope it was thrown away and not sold to a used furniture store!

When I was at school, I couldn't focus on the things the teacher wanted me to because I was worried about running out of underwear and whether or not Mom would find my hidden sheets. I'm sad to say that I had teachers who tried the same tactics that Dad did to change my behavior. Rewards and punishments had the same effect on me at school as they did at home. More attempts, more failures, more shame.

The biggest gift we can give kids is to act like we don't know that they are smelly and scared and poor. We need to make them feel safe and loved and valued. That's the only way to end the legacy of shame.

The Night My Father Died

We were living in Pomona, KS the night my father died. Dad had been working several jobs so my brother and I were helping him with one of those projects, sealing the roofs of mobile homes in the area. We were using a process called cool sealing that involved mopping the tops of trailers with a waterproof sealant that cost about $50 for a five gallon bucket. To maximize profits, Dad thinned the product with diesel fuel so he could get twice as much sealant for almost the same price. Of course our customers were getting ripped off because the waterproofing ability was also cut in half, but that's what he had us doing in the hot Kansas summer sun for $8.00 a day. It was hot, hard work, and I got the worst sunburn of my life on top of those mobile homes, but that pain paled in comparison to the pain I was about to experience.

One night after work, Dad decided we should all go to a keg party at Pomona Lake. Even though we didn't know the bikers and other characters who invited him very well, the offer of free beer was all Dad needed to hear so we headed to the lake. As you can imagine, the night got pretty wild. I won't go into details, but I will say it wasn't a good night to be my dad's son. I did a pretty good job keeping an eye on Dad since I didn't drink, and this wasn't the first time his behavior had forced me into a role reversal. However, even a surrogate father has his limits, so the third time Dad got his truck stuck driving in the sand at the edge of the lake, I decided I'd had enough. I saw another family getting ready to leave so I asked them if I could have a ride. They didn't live in Pomona, but they offered to let me spend the night at their house. When I woke up the next morning, the first thought I had was, "Dad's dead." I knew it. The minute I woke up I knew it.

I begged the family to give me a ride back to Pomona, and when I got home, the somber faces and bowed heads of my family confirmed my premonition. My brother said, "Do you know dad drowned?" The coroner ruled out a heart attack, and my brother said Dad was sober by the time he decided to go for a swim so there was no explanation for how such a strong swimmer could drown in waist deep water. I struggled for answers, for closure. My dad could swim like a fish. He could swim across the lake. I'd never seen anyone who was a stronger swimmer.

Then I realized that no explanation was going to assuage the guilt I felt. I abandoned my post. My job was to watch dad, to keep him safe, and I had failed miserably. I continued to blame myself for years until I had a child of my own. That's when I finally understood that a 16-year-old boy shouldn't have the job of being his dad's dad. That should never have been my responsibility. That's when I decided to use the adversity in my life as the inspiration to build something good. It's not easy to channel those negative memories and emotions in a positive direction, but you have to break free and do something good in spite of the circumstances you've been given. Dad made some poor choices on the night he died, but I can build a better future for me and my family by making the right ones.

Locked out of the Motel Room

The early memories of my childhood are hard to put on a timeline. Was I three or was I four when this or that happened? I suppose it really doesn't matter, but I can usually remember if I had started school or not, and this one is definitely a pre-K memory. It was one of those times when we were on the road with Dad, and Mom wasn't around. Those were always dangerous times when we were left without a protector. We were staying in a motel room, and Dad was drinking. Dad was being Dad, and I was being a kid, which meant I was irritating him. I don't remember what my crime was, but I will never forget my punishment. Dad put me outside the motel room and locked door.

I knew I was in trouble when I heard the click of the deadbolt lock. I'd been locked out of the house before so I knew that pounding on the door would only make things worse. I looked around and immediately noticed the neon lights that outlined the silhouette of the building. Back then the glowing pink and blue lights served as a beacon to weary travelers. They were garish things that still lured you off the highway with a kind of decadent beauty. I'm sure I would have been even more terrified without those lights to soften the darkness, but they were little comfort to my young mind as I grasped the gravity of my situation. It was just me and the crickets and the rest of the world. As I sat out there crying for what seemed like hours, I realized that I was alone and at the mercy of the world. That kind of abandonment makes a deep impression on a young child. It wrote deeply and vividly on my mind, heart, and soul.

I was crying loudly enough to bother the other guests so they called the manager, and he made my dad let me back in the room. I never think of that experience without thinking about the kids that come to school without a feeling of safety and security. If you don't feel safe, you can't learn. If you don't feel safe, you are just surviving day to day. When I became a teacher, I worked hard to create a safe space where kids knew they were not going to be attacked. They had a place where they could belong. The best gift we can give kids who come from poverty or kids who come from chaos, or any kid for that matter, is a safe place with expectations and norms. As much as they act like they don't want these things, they absolutely need that safety and that security. So I learned that night that it's a big, scary world when you are alone so we have to find a way to open the door for kids who need to come in from the darkness.

Cathy and the Facts of Honeycutt Life

The facts of life are hard for all of us to accept at times. We all experience pain, both physical and emotional. It's unavoidable. Unsuccessful people let that pain consume and control them. Successful people take that pain and turn it into something positive. This story is one of the most difficult childhood memories I have, but I tell it as an ode to the sister I never knew. I now have three sisters, Angie, Sandy and Lorie, and I love them very much. They are all great people, but I had another sister named Cathy who lives in my memory as a little China doll because she was so young when she died. Even though my time with Cathy was very brief, her death taught me what it takes to survive.

Cathy might have been a little premature when she was born, but I was so young that many of the details from that time are gone from my memory. I do know that she was only a few weeks old when she got sick, and her illness coincided with my dad's decision to relocate the family. When he decided to load everyone in the car to go on to the next golden sunshine place that would fix his life, there was no way to talk him out of it. He always thought that a fresh start was the answer to all his problems. He used up places, and he used up people and those actions demanded that we hit the road again. Unfortunately, that meant taking Cathy on the road in a car with no heater. I remember wondering why our baby doll that mom bought wouldn't stop coughing. In a motel room one night near San Antonio, Texas, Cathy died. Years later I surmised that she had pneumonia, but the only thing I knew back then was that Mom and Dad were talking about some serious stuff the next morning.

Cathy was in an unmarked grave for many years, and my mom always dreamed about buying her a grave marker. Eventually she was able to do that so Cathy finally had a headstone to show the world that she had lived, no matter how briefly, as a member of the Honeycutt family. Cathy's death was a cautionary tale that taught me to hold on tightly to life. Believing that the weak got left behind made me stronger, but it was also a difficult way to live. When I work with kids living in poverty, my message to them is SURVIVE. Survive and persist until you're 18, and then your life is your own. Hang in there with everything you have. Use your pain as a motivating force to achieve things beyond anyone's expectation of you. That's what I've always tried to do as a way to honor Cathy and her life that was taken from us too soon.

Driving Full Circle

I turned 16 the year my father died, and I was working at the cement plant lifting heavy bags of concrete all day long to earn some money. I drove a Toyota Celica that I paid $200 for, and it was definitely a $200 car. I think I must have been working off the books because I didn't get a regular paycheck. Someone would hand me $30 in cash here and there, and that was enough to keep oil in my car. Yes, I said oil in my car, not gas, because every ten miles I would have to stop and add oil to the engine because that's how much it burned up or leaked out. Leaking oil wasn't the only problem with my car. To start it, you had to open the hood, force open the carburetor with a rag wrapped in string, crank the engine, and yank the rag out really fast once the car started. I never thought too much about what my dream car was, but that was about to change.

I also worked for Job Corps in addition to my time at the cement plant so occasionally I had to go to the Corps of Engineers office at Pomona Lake for training. One day I decided to take the country back roads for a change of scenery, and as I was driving, I caught a glimpse of something in the grass. I must have had a vision because somehow I knew that rusty piece of metal sticking out of the tall grass was the rear quarter panel of a '69 Camaro. I drove on to my training, but I made a mental note of where this farm was, and on the way back, I stopped and knocked at the door. "Is that a '69 Camaro?" I nervously asked the man who answered the door.

"Yes, my grandson totaled it, and he left it here years ago. It might be yours if you want it," he responded.

I asked if I could look at the car, and to my delight I discovered that the car was in perfect condition from the front door to the back, I mean perfect: a small block 327 bored out for racing and a 12 bolt 4.11 Positrack, 350 turbo automatic with a B & M shift kit, US racing slots all around, 50 series tires on the back, 70s on the front all "Revengers." This was one bad car fed by a 750 double pumper Holley carburetor. I knew this stuff, but if you don't, let me just say it was a sweet ride with an emphasis on the WAS because the front end had been driven through a house. So I asked, "How much for the car?" The man said he wanted $450 for it, which was a good price since the engine was worth more than that. I asked him if I could make payments, and the deal was struck. My $30 here and there from the cement plant along with my pay from Job Corps and anything else I could scrape together from friends went toward that rusting vehicular dream sitting in the grass near Pomona Lake.

Finally, the day arrived when it was all mine, and I made arrangements to pull that car home. That's when my obsession began. That car became everything to me for three years. Every minute I wasn't working, I was looking for parts. I found a part here and a part there until I had two new fenders. Then I found a bumper. Piece by piece I worked until I had the front end restored. Then I primed and sanded the body so it was all ready to paint. I put new carpet on the inside and hand-painted a mural on the fender well. I painted the engine orange, and it was so clean you could have eaten dinner off it. I didn't have much in my life, but I had this dream, this car that I was going to drive to prom my senior year.

It was a great dream. I could clearly see myself pulling up with my date in my metallic midnight blue '69 Camaro with silver rally stripes, but that never happened. I came so close, and it wasn't for lack of effort. I just ran out of time. Then that August, college started. I had scholarships that covered my tuition and meals, but I had no money for books or any incidentals. The only thing of value I had was my Camaro. As painful as it was, I started selling parts of my car.

I started with the carburetor. It was worth a few hundred dollars so my carburetor became my first books at college. Tearing the car apart piece by piece started to tear me apart so I knew I had to sell what was left intact. I felt like I'd lost a family member as I watched my car drive away.

I don't know if everyone has that kind of relationship with the first car that they love, but I was heart-broken. Fortunately, life goes on, and I finished college, married my wife, and had a child. I became a teacher, and then I became an educational consultant. Once things were better financially, I had a new vision of what our next car should be. Even though I still dreamed about that Camaro, I knew that shouldn't be our next vehicle.

When I met my wife, Michele, she was driving a Plymouth Duster with a 318. I fell in love with her because of the way she popped that clutch. There was something so rock 'n roll about the way she drove that car. So a few years ago, I found the new

Dodge Challenger, and I thought that it looked like her old Duster. I took Michele to the car lot and we came home with her dream car. I'm a little slow to learn some lessons, but this is one I took to heart a long time ago, and it has served me well: Always take care of her first. Her dream needs to be your dream. She loved her car so much, and not surprisingly, it didn't take long for her to say, "Go get your car." Fortunately, that year the 2010 Camaro came out and it looked like the '69. It was so cool. I didn't go crazy and buy a brand new one with the V8. Instead, I bought a used one with some miles on it and a V6 engine, but I had my car!

Before I sold the '69 Camaro, I took Michele for a country drive in it. We had been dating for a while, and I thought I could impress her with this cool car I rebuilt. Unfortunately, the car died several times because I'd sold the good carburetor and replaced it with a piece of junk. Out of embarrassment and frustration, I hit the windshield and broke it. Losing your mind in front of the girl you think you might marry someday is not something I would recommend, but luckily I didn't scare her off so we were able to go back to that same eastern Kansas road with the new Camaro and finish our romantic drive. It was one of the coolest moments in my life.

I had to wait a long time to finish that drive, but I realized that if I was patient, things can come full circle. Instead of taking out a loan that I couldn't afford while I was in school, I waited. This ability to forestall the things you want, to hold on, to wait, and to do it right, that's the difference between success and failure. Yes, I'm a gnarled, old man now driving a

2010 Camaro, but when I drive it I'm sixteen again, and that's what really matters.

Sub-tropic Tan: The Florida Story

If you live north of the Mason-Dixon line, you've probably dreamed about moving south and finding a place on the beach, at least during the winter months. Sitting in a chaise lounge sipping a drink with an umbrella beats shoveling snow for almost everyone. However, there is another side to Florida that most tourists never see, but I experienced a tropical stay many years ago that was anything but idyllic.

Our move to Florida was one of those crazy times when Dad decided to pack everyone in the car and head out without any employment, money, or plans. Somehow he convinced Uncle Larry and his family to come along so we had two cars, a truck and a Volkswagon Beetle in our caravan, and we were headed to the Promised Land to strike it rich. The sad truth was that we were totally unprepared for the reality of Florida.

The drive itself was exhausting, and when we finally made it to Florida, we went from town to town looking for work. With no money, we ended up living in the worst trailer parks in the world with no air conditioning and roaches the size of your foot. None of us were ready for the Florida heat and humidity, but it hit Dad worst of all because he did construction work and roofing. As a result, we ended up living in several different towns while Dad searched for work that was a little less brutal than construction. One of those towns was Daytona Beach.

When most people hear Daytona Beach, they think " Ahh...Daytona Beach." It was never that way for us. We never stayed at the great hotels and resorts that the city had to offer. We ended up in a ramshackle trailer in a dismal trailer park. Dad was drinking because he was angry about his life and the poor choices he'd made. While he was partying, Mom would be home alone with us, and dangerous people were doing dangerous things right outside our door. Sometimes the danger came inside as it did the night Dad came home drunk and hit Mom. She called the abuse hotline, and we ended up at a shelter for a while. I don't know how long we were at the shelter, but eventually we ended up back at the trailer park. We might not have stayed at the resorts on the beach, but late at night we were close enough to see the bright lights and listen to the ads for Sub-tropic Tan suntan oil that blared from the tourists' radios. You could even smell the scent of suntan oil in the air, and I knew I was so close to something really cool.

I want to go back there and enjoy Daytona Beach in a way I never could as a child. I can do that now because I developed a plan. It is really hard to build a life if you don't have a plan. It's not going to just happen for you. I'm teaching my kids that success is a combination of hard work, planning, and time. That's what really makes a life.

Messin' with Crazy

Growing up in a family where some of the people were behaviorally unpredictable, I knew there was a difference between someone who had a mental disorder and someone who consciously chose to live outside the norms of society. What took some time to learn was how to tell the difference. There are many variations of this kind of unpredictable behavior, but in my personal experience, the ones with a clinical diagnosis were less dangerous than someone who was just plain mean because people in the latter group were always ready to escalate any conflict, and you were never sure where they would stop. When I was a seventh grader, my love for karate put me at the mercy of an individual who definitely fit into one of those two categories.

We were still living in our ghetto apartment in New Windsor, Maryland when I got involved in karate. I studied it, talked about it, and connected with people who knew something about it so I could learn from them. I met a man who lived in our apartment building, and he mentioned that he knew a specific type of karate that was unfamiliar to me. I was curious and said casually, "Do you want to spar?" To me, sparring meant fighting at a low level without pads so no one would get hurt. I'm not sure what sparring meant to him when he was sober, but when he was drunk it obviously meant something quite different.

We went upstairs to his apartment, and his first hit threw me against the wall. My head broke through the plaster. Caving in the wall wasn't my idea of sparring. That's when I realized he wasn't going to hold back. It was on. I was in a real fight, and it wasn't going to end well for me. Looking back I realize it could have been much worse. He was drunk and out of shape so that limited the amount of energy he could exert on my beating. I put several more holes in the wall before he finally got tired of knocking me around, and I went downstairs. I never told anyone about this incident because I was embarrassed that I got my butt kicked when I thought I was pretty good at karate. The reality was that if I'd told someone, this guy would have been arrested.

Something good came out of the experience because I learned to avoid crazy. It was my first lesson in spotting someone who was willing to take something to another level. If you are trying to build a better life for yourself, look around and sniff the air. If it feels like a bad place where people might do bad things, get out. Hanging out with people who don't have boundaries to their behavior is just messin' with crazy.

The Power of Believing

"What the mind of man can conceive and believe, it can achieve." This quote by Napoleon Hill, an early author of personal success, or self-help, literature has been used many times to highlight the importance of self-confidence. It's cute, it rhymes, and it's completely true. If you can conceptualize a possible outcome and believe that it lies within the realm of possibility, you are likely to achieve success. Without that belief, failure is likely. I learned just how true the statement is when I was in the eighth grade.

As an eighth grader with underdeveloped frontal lobes, it's no surprise that I got into an argument with an older kid. He was in ninth grade. He wasn't any more emotionally developed than I was, but his biceps certainly were. He was also about a foot taller than me so you might think I would just walk away when he started saying inappropriate things, and you would be wrong. I had my reaction button on my forehead, and he was only too happy to push it. The argument quickly escalated into a shouting match, and he wanted to fight right there in the cafeteria. As the new kid at school, I knew I had to avoid the scenario where he had the whole school cheering him on. Additionally, since it was obvious that a severe beating was in my future, I had to figure out a way to make this as private as possible so I said, "No, I'll fight you, but it will be just you and me in the bathroom."

I met him in the bathroom, and we both started throwing punches. At least I think I punched a little in the beginning. It becomes a little surreal when you're getting completely thrashed by someone. Somehow during one of my attempts at self-preservation, we were locked together wrestling. As he pushed me away, his hand caught on the little crucifix necklace my girlfriend had given me. I felt the chain snap and watched the little cross fall to the bathroom floor.

When he broke my necklace, something happened in my head. My brain screamed, "You broke my necklace! My girlfriend gave me that!" Suddenly, I wasn't afraid anymore. My shift from defense to offense took him completely by surprise, and my anger pushed me into another gear. I was the one landing the blows and inflicting pain. At some point we both mutually agreed that we'd had enough, and the fight ended in a handshake. We both had swollen lips and a little blood on our clothes, but nothing that prevented us from going back to class.

Now I'm not advocating that anyone go out and pick a fight as a strategy to develop self-confidence. I use this story to illustrate the point that I was losing because I didn't think I could win. That's the way it is in life most of the time. You can do as well as you think you can. Since you're as powerful as you think you are, why not go ahead and believe in yourself?

Faulty Wiring

Dad taught me a lot of things I had to unlearn as an adult. One of those things was that the police were bad. Cops were our enemies. The other thing he taught me was bigotry. I totally understand how ironic it was that we judged other people when we had absolutely nothing, but that's how I was wired, and it made some of the situations Dad got us into very difficult to navigate.

One night Dad took us on one of his scary hell rides after a big fight with Mom. He loaded all the kids in the car to punish her because he knew it would scare her to have us out on the road with him when he was drunk. I don't know how scared she was, but we were all terrified. Fortunately, it didn't take long for the police lights to come on so Dad told us to hide the beer cans because the evil police were coming. Dad got arrested and charged with DWI, that's a DUI in today's terminology, so he went to jail, and we got to come along for the ride. I still feel sorry for the poor policeman who had to deal with us that night. As we got out of the car, we were all holding on to dad like monkeys clinging to their mom in some National Geographic special. The policeman peeled us off one at a time, and when he grabbed me, I bit him. I don't mean I went after him half-heartedly. I mean I took a bite out of his hand. I wish I could find the officer and apologize, but I'm sure I wasn't the first child who was taught to hate the police.

After Dad got booked, the policeman took us to a foster home that night, and the family we stayed with was black. I was terrified to get out of the car because of all the things I had been taught. I gave the policeman as good a chase as I could in the confines of a police car, but eventually he got me into the house. To my surprise, the family was very nice. They bought us clothes and toys, and they didn't do any of the things I had been told they would do.

I used to look back on those times and wish I'd been a nicer kid and wish I hadn't bitten the cop and wish I hadn't been a tiny bigot. Now I understand that I just had faulty wiring, and I have the rest of my life to fix all those things. The important thing to remember is that just because you are told something, doesn't mean it's true. If you find yourself constantly disagreeing with the beliefs of others or feeling like you are the odd man out in many situations, maybe it's time to see about getting some new wiring.

Ode to My Siblings

In any toxic childhood, your life is like shooting the rapids in a rubber raft. Everyone is holding on for dear life and praying to come out the other side. That's how it was for my siblings and me. We were all focused on surviving. Living in such a tumultuous situation made it difficult to have the strength to reach out and lift up another person. However, there were moments of grace in my childhood when we did reach out, and we helped each other. As I look at my brother and sisters, I'm filled with love and admiration for their journey. I'm also filled with gratitude to them for sharing the journey with me.

My brother, Carl, was the oldest so he was there to welcome me home when I was born. Carl was tough from the very beginning, and he could fight even though he wasn't very big when he was younger. The guy just had a strength that came from somewhere, somewhere deep inside, which meant he could handle himself in any situation. I give Carl credit for making me tough by beating me up often. I am serious when I say that because I wasn't naturally tough like Carl. I was more like Mom with a softer side and less ability to stand up for myself. Just because he was tough didn't mean Carl had an easy road. He was close to my dad, and being close to Dad wasn't the gift it sounds like. Dad attempted to make Carl in his own image, and Carl suffered for that. Carl is immensely creative, with more artistic ability than I have. He is also the person I want around if a fight breaks out because all I have to do is whistle and he will be there. With Carl on your side, everything will be okay. I wouldn't be the person I am today if he hadn't been in my life.

My sister, Sandy, was injured in the big explosion that gutted our house in Woodbine, Maryland. She was the only family member with life threatening injuries, and she made her way back from all of that with a lot of physical therapy. She has gone on to have this amazingly cool life with some great kids of her own. Her triumph over the physical adversity and pain she suffered has always been an inspiration to me.

My next sister, Angela, was an amazing friend to me because our personalities are very similar. We would play and talk for hours imagining we were somewhere else living any kind of life we could envision. She is a sensitive soul and a really sweet person. It makes me so happy to see her life now because things are going well. She's finally finding the happiness she deserves.

Lorie, who is the baby of the family, is perhaps the wisest of us all or maybe she just had the benefit of learning from our mistakes. She saw what worked and what didn't, and she became this very intelligent person who is fun, honest, and direct. I don't have to worry about Mom because I know Lorie is close by looking after her.

It's amazing to me that we could all get to the other side of all the darkness in our lives as children. It took a while for us to emerge, and we did it in different ways. I know it's been hard for all of us, but I love my brother and sisters, and I thank them for every time they helped me hang on and dream of a happier future. I believe the best times are still ahead for all of us.

Coming Attractions

One of the skills necessary to achieve a successful life is the ability to anticipate the outcomes of an action before they happen. It would be nice if life had a Preview button or a Coming Attractions trailer we could watch. Unfortunately, things aren't that simple as I learned the hard way in a little town called Leary, Texas.

I used to come home from school every day and walk the railroad tracks since there wasn't much else to do for entertainment. Sometimes there would be railroad spikes just lying around or sticking out loosely from the tracks. I would collect these railroad spikes and keep them in a 5-gallon bucket. I don't know why, but I found these railroad spikes terribly interesting. One day it occurred to me that it might be fun to hit these spikes with my aluminum baseball bat. I have no clue where this idea originated, but this is the point where the Preview button would have been very helpful.

The spikes would make an incredible sound as the caromed off the bat, and they would fly through the air like rockets. The bat would vibrate in my hands in a way that felt almost electric. I'm not sure why the activity felt so therapeutic, but I enjoyed it immensely. One day I came home from school, and it had been a particularly challenging day so I really needed to hit a few spikes to relieve the tension. I threw the first spike up into the air, and I released a vicious swing that I knew was going to create an amazing pulsation through my body when the bat and railroad spike collided. Just before I made contact, I looked out across the field to find that someone had moved a new trailer right behind our house while I was at school. I knew I couldn't stop my swing, but I prayed that I could stop the spike telepathically. Unfortunately, no amount of prayer, wishing, or telekinesis could deter the projectile as it flew toward the structure. It went right through the side ripping a gaping hole. I couldn't believe the damage my little spike created because I wasn't that well versed in mobile home construction. I now know my feat was akin to throwing a rock at toilet paper.

Of course the homeowner was furious, and once my mom and dad got involved, a good whipping was inevitable. The most painful part of the experience was the feeling I had mid-swing when I knew this terrible thing was about to happen, and I was powerless to stop it. That feeling has stayed with me, and it helps to guide my decisions to this day. I try to anticipate all possible scenarios by asking, "What will the result be if I do this?" By checking out the Coming Attractions, I'm in control if it's a movie I don't want to see.

One Man's Trash

Living in a New Windsor, Maryland slum apartment was ground zero for me. By that I mean life was bleak. I don't know how else to describe it. The winter months when we couldn't stay outside were hard times. I was struggling through middle school without decent clothes to wear and very little to eat. Every day that I went to school, I knew there was a good chance that someone was going to make fun of me for what I was wearing or how I acted. With so little going right in my life, I had to use every opportunity to get ahead, even if that included repurposing someone else's trash.

I didn't have many marketable skills at this point in my life, but I was always a tinkerer, a fixer. If something was broken, I could usually fix it 9 times out of 10. One day I was dumpster diving, and I found a broken 8-track tape player, the first boombox. It was a Panasonic—a Panasonic 8-track that required 8 C batteries! Finding the money for 8 batteries was a challenge, but somehow I amassed enough cash to purchase them. I carefully pried the case open and discovered that the belt had slipped off of the drive. I stuck the belt back on and suddenly I had a Panasonic 8-track Boombox! Me—the guy who was living in the slum apartments. Of course I was now the hit of the school! I took my boombox to recess, but I had to choose my moments carefully because once I popped an 8-track in, it ate those batteries pretty fast. I had to make sure the moment was right before I got the party started.

I was repurposing and recycling things before it became an environmental necessity. Even now when I can afford to buy a new item, I never feel too proud to fix something someone else discarded. I never fail to see the value in something that someone else thought was worthless. In the beginning I did it out of necessity. Now I do it because it's cool to turn trash into treasure.

Hero/Anti-Hero

I've often thought about who was the bigger influence in my life, Mom or Dad. Mom had all the good qualities I wanted to emulate, but most of Dad's actions served as a cautionary tale for me. I finally decided that even though Dad's lessons in what NOT to do were valuable, the things I truly learned from him were mostly things I've spent my adulthood trying to fix. I feel that 99% of the person I am today is because of my mom, and the 1% of what I've had to overcome was from my dad. Because of her love and self-sacrifice, Mom has always been my hero. I guess all the things I learned not to do from Dad make him the anti-hero.

Mom taught me how to be a good person through her actions rather than words. Some of the most powerful lessons from my childhood, I learned through her pain. When Mom cried, I knew Dad was doing the wrong thing. Even before I was old enough to be aware of what was going on, Mom suffered on behalf of her children. Whatever it took to hold this family together, she did it. She hung in there like grim death. Countless times she tied a rag around her head and cleaned the current dump Dad moved us into. She would clean it with Spick and Span and Pinesol so it always smelled clean, even if it looked terrible. She would get out her "whatnots" and strategically arrange them so it seemed like home again. Mom could re-set what seemed like home anywhere.

She gave herself completely to being a Mom and worked her fingers to the bone. If money was really tight, Dad would let her work part time to make ends meet, but he never let her work full time. I always thought that if she had a career, she might have an identity and enough independence to break free, but that never happened until after Dad died. Then Mom had to work because she had all these kids to feed and rent to pay. She got a job as a janitress, Google that if you don't believe it's a real word, and she was the best one that had ever worked, or will ever work, at Pomona Schools. I'm just going to say that flat out. Mom could do the job. She could strip a floor and wax it to perfection. I used to help her in the summers, and I saw people come and go in that position, but none of them could do the job like Mom because she cared about her work. One thing I learned from her was to take pride in everything you do, even if it's cleaning toilets. I do that with everything I do now.

Mom would come home tired with little pay for her efforts, and then she had all the other stuff to do that kept the family going. Everything that I am today is because of Mom's sacrifice. I will never forget that. I love you Mom, and I hope someday you will read this and know the debt of gratitude I can never repay. You'll always be my hero.

Sharing Your Gifts

Twenty-three years ago, my wife and I were anxiously awaiting the birth of our first child. We didn't know if we were having a boy or a girl, and we couldn't wait to find out. Michele's due date assigned by the doctor was November 12th, but we were both sure that calculation was wrong so we weren't surprised when she started having contractions on the evening of October 14th. Feeling both excited and scared, we got our things together and headed to the hospital. The hospital we drove to wasn't the one we were supposed to deliver in, but we decided we didn't want to chance making the longer drive since we didn't know how fast her labor would progress. After arriving at the emergency room, the doctor examined her and determined that she was indeed in labor. Because she was a month early (by their calculations), the doctors eventually decided to stop the labor with a drug called Brethine. Her contractions slowed and then stopped completely so we headed home. We tried to ease our disappointment by saying it was undoubtedly for the best for him/her to delay the birth.

The next evening I asked my wife if I could draw our yet unseen child on her protruding belly to help me better visualize the impending offspring. She replied quickly and vehemently, "No!" Three days later, despite the Brethine, she started having contractions, and once again we leapt into Go Mode. We quickly gathered our things and drove the 40 miles to the hospital that we were scheduled to deliver in. Upon checking in and getting examined, the doctor determined that Michele was in early labor. She was feeling some serious back pain, and the doctor suggested we walk around to help relieve it. As we walked, I massaged her bulging belly to encourage the labor along. After six hours, the contractions slowed down and her labor eventually stopped altogether. Once again we drove home disappointed.

I am not what you would call a patient person. I have always had a hard time understanding the concept of delayed gratification. As a child, it was always torture for me to wait until Christmas day to open my presents. This baby was like a giant wrapped present I had been waiting to open for far too long so a week later I again timidly broached the subject of the belly drawing. This time Michele surprised me by saying yes. She was either taking pity on me, or her need to visualize the growing person inside her outweighed any embarrassment of serving as my canvas.

Excitedly I gathered my supplies. I finally had the chance I was hoping for, and believe me, I was ready. At the doctor's office, while waiting for our doctor to appear, the two of us passed the time by gazing at posters depicting children in utero. I didn't realize this study in anatomy was preparing me to complete what I consider to be my greatest work of art. In addition, I had an active imagination and four years experience as an art instructor. In short, I came to this challenge almost as well prepared as Michelangelo before he began painting the Sistine Chapel. "Will it come off easily," my wife asked nervously as I prepared to make the first stroke. "Of course," I answered. "These are water-based markers. It will all disappear with a little soap and water."

I began by drawing the uterus (people who haven't had children or are squeamish may choose to stop reading here), and I then proceeded to the child itself. I drew the umbilical cord and capped it all off with the placenta. I used several colors and articulated finite details such as veins and eye lashes. It isn't bragging to say the final work was a very realistic rendering of a child in utero. Michele and I looked at her belly in amazement. Neither of us could speak for a moment because the image of our baby moved us to tears. I went to sleep happy that night, knowing that my artistic skills had enabled us to visualize the child we both longed to see.

At around 12:30 a.m., Michele woke me to say that her water had broken. After a happy hug, she immediately turned her attention to the masterpiece on her midsection. "I'm taking a shower," she said. "You load the car." I had just come back in after taking the suitcases out when I heard my name called, or more accurately, screamed. Worriedly I raced into the bathroom to encounter my wife, standing in the shower, frantically scrubbing her belly with a back-brush. "It's not coming off," she said, with a wild look in her eyes. I was so relieved that she was okay that I stood for a moment at the bathroom door laughing at her predicament. Wrong move. A tip for fathers-to-be out there: Never laugh at a woman in labor, especially one holding a back-brush!

After 20 minutes of scrubbing, soaping, and loofah-ing my wife, it was evident to me that my artwork was going to be seen by a few more people than we'd intended. After another 40 minutes of Michele declaring that she wasn't going to the hospital with my artwork on her belly, I finally convinced her that I couldn't deliver the baby so she got into the car. I like to think that threatening to carry her to the car did the trick (not an easy feat to bluff about since she'd gain 50 pounds), but actually it was probably the increasing intensity of the labor pains that forced her to acquiesce.

Secretly I was happy about our inability to remove my drawing. This was my artwork, and I wanted other people to see it. I'm sorry, but I'm an artist, and we like to share our gifts. To my delight, my artwork was the hit of the hospital! In fact the baby "on" her belly seemed to interest everyone as much as the one "in" her belly. Word quickly spread throughout the hospital, and a steady flow of doctors, nurses, janitors and cafeteria workers popped in to "take a peek" at my masterpiece. Let me say this about the whole affair, it evokes much more humor from my wife today than it did at the time.

After 12 hours of labor, we were able to see our beautiful baby boy in the flesh. He was a healthy 8 pounds, 6 ounces and looked much like we'd pictured him earlier. My art, on the other hand, looked quite deflated. My most memorable work to date had been destroyed. And then my new Magnum Opus was placed in my arms, and I couldn't wait to share this amazing gift with the world.

Learning How to Learn

When I arrived on campus for the first time, I had to make the same adjustments to college life that many freshmen go through: homesickness, disorientation, and loneliness. I got through high school easily, largely because expectations for me were pretty low. I'm not blaming my teachers. I wouldn't have been anyone's pick as "most likely to succeed" from my class, but the easy path I took in high school didn't serve me well once I graduated. I realized early in my college experience that I had an additional obstacle to overcome. I had to learn how to learn.

I was never officially diagnosed with a learning disability, but reading was a struggle for me. Just decoding the text was difficult enough, but comprehension was where I really struggled. I had to read every assignment three times and take notes each time. I had to stay up most of the night reviewing just to keep the material in my head. It was frustrating, almost excruciating at times, but I was not leaving, and I was not getting kicked out for poor grades! I knew I had to hang in there. If I was going to change my life, I had to stay and that meant keeping my grades up.

By Christmas, classes were getting a little easier. There were still some places where I struggled, but I persevered and had mostly A's, and B's, with an occasional C, over the next six years. Changing majors a couple of times added the two extra years, but I finished! I was proud of my accomplishment, but I was even prouder of the fact that I had transformed myself into a lifelong learner. That's the message that I share with students. Don't make excuses for yourself by blaming others for the lack of preparation you might have had. At the end of the day, the person you become is up to you.

All Night Paint Job

My dad had trouble making good decisions his entire life, in large part due to his drinking and drug use, and that was never more apparent than when he decided he was a car painter. His main qualification for becoming a car painter was his purchase of a Wagner Power Painter. He painted a couple of fences first, which gave him the confidence to make the move to automotive painting, and he convinced his step-dad to let him paint his Ford LTD. Since Grandpa could hardly see, that probably wasn't a bad place to start.

As was the case with most of his wild ideas, all the children were expected to help paint this car. Unfortunately, he was taking a powerful stimulant called Plegine, which allowed him to function for days at a time without any sleep, and he expected us to stay up with him when we were working on a project. We didn't have the help of any stimulant drugs. We were just normal human beings who were forced to stay awake as long as he wanted to work.

The first job he gave us was to sand the car. We worked hard all day thinking we might get to quit when it got dark. Instead, Dad put up a couple of lights and pulled out the power painter. If you've ever used a power painter, you know that the tip of the painter is critical to the success of the project. It disperses the paint in an even coat that eliminates runs and drips, ensuring a smooth finish. Well, that piece broke. It broke shortly after he started, so at two o'clock in the morning in Brushtown,

Pennsylvania, Dad decided we were going to invent a tip for a Wagner Power Painter.

We stayed up all night searching for every bottle cap in the house and drilling into it to try to make a sort of port that would distribute the paint evenly. The first attempts were terrible because when we started painting the car, the paint just poured out in a single stream. Then we had to wipe all of that paint off and try again. We made many of those homemade tips in an effort to find one that would work correctly. By 5:00 a.m., I was trying to get my brother to take a shift so I could sleep, but it was every man for himself at this point. Dad was excited and whistling and having a great time because he was still high on his drug, but we were dying a million deaths.

Somehow in the middle of this chaos, my dad got distracted from the work on the car and decided to refinish my mom's guitar. Maybe he saw the futility in what we were doing, and he decided to move on to another impossible task. Regardless of his motivation, he took the guitar that Mom really liked, and he started sanding off the finish. Once he had the old finish removed, he realized he had nothing to use for a stain so he found a bottle of Mecurochrome and poured it on the guitar. The Mercurochrome actually looked pretty good on the guitar, and Dad might have pulled this off if he had stopped there. Unfortunately, he decided to hand paint a rose on the guitar. Now my father was a great con artist but never a real artist. However, on Plegine he thought he could do anything. So he painted this red blob on the guitar that looked more like a bullet wound than a rose, and Mom was extremely unhappy when she saw the finished product.

To escape the ensuing argument, Dad headed back out to the car project. At this time, he said to forget using the power painter. We could just paint it with a roller. So we painted the whole car with a roller because Dad surmised that Grandpa wouldn't be able to see details anyway. But, you could feel it. The finish felt like the skin of an orange, and I was appalled that my dad was satisfied with such a shoddy job. It was one thing to cheat strangers by selling them green wood to burn, but this was family.

When you are just a kid, you are usually powerless to change the circumstances you see around you, and that was certainly the case with the paint job on Grandpa's car. However, that experience taught me that when you do have a choice, you can walk away from people who are doing things you don't like. When you see someone on a course of destruction doing the absolute wrong thing, you can step off. It's your life. You can step off and do your own thing or join someone else who has something going on that is actually leading somewhere. Just because someone in your life engages in self-destructive behavior doesn't mean you have to join him or her in the activity. You get to choose. Once I became an adult, I was very careful about the people I chose to follow because I realized my life was like a blank canvas, and I wanted to paint something beautiful.

Front Row Seat

My dad died right before my freshman year at Pomona High School, and to say I was struggling with my classes that year would be a huge understatement. I made C's and D's because I just wasn't trying. Nothing in my life seemed to matter at that point, particularly school. I felt like a spectator, rather than a participant, in my own life, and I didn't even have a very good view. I had no idea that the solution to my problems was within me, and all I had to do was choose a front row seat.

I was sitting in class in the back row. Isn't that where everyone who has difficulty learning wants to sit? That's the place where teachers leave you alone if you leave them alone. I was so bored that I was literally hitting my head against the wall. It was a traditional cinder block wall, and I wasn't hitting my head very hard, just enough to be a little numb. I whispered "boring, boring, boring," to myself until I accidentally hit my head a little too hard against the wall. I felt my brain hit the side of my skull, and I had a vision of my own future.

There I was in my single-wide trailer without skirting. My kids didn't have shoes, and I was repeating the life that I came from. A voice inside me said, "No, no I don't want that to be me!" In that instant, I got up and walked to the front of the room to an available seat, and I sat in one of those empty chairs. And my life changed that day.

I knew that the teachers cared about the kids who sat in the front seats, and I desperately needed someone to care about me. The teachers also asked those kids more questions, and it would be embarrassing if I didn't know the answers. So I started looking at the book to find out why the kids in the front row seats knew all the answers, and I didn't. One thing I realized when I started paying attention was that the next right answer during class discussion was often the next **dark black** word in the book. Once I solved that mystery, I started answering questions, and then I started reading ahead and memorizing the dark black words. That's when I started acing the quizzes and tests. I wasn't stupid; I just had to break the code.

When I speak to teachers and administrators, I challenge them to engage and empower every student. Technology has made that easier to do than ever before. Cell phones, iPads, and laptops provide the opportunity for children to be in charge of their own learning. They can all learn and interact with the class in ways that don't embarrass them or make them feel left out. The shy kids can blossom, and the bored kids can stop banging their heads against the wall. It's time to move everyone to a front row seat.

Spread Your Wings

In my first year teaching, I taught in Ottawa, Kansas. I taught at five elementary schools with over 1500 kids in my classes. I took art on a cart to all of those schools, and I learned a lot from that job because I had the opportunity to observe other teachers and how they handled their classrooms. If you get to work in that many grade schools with that many teachers, you are exposed to a lot of expertise and a lot of different teaching styles. That unique experience really shaped the teacher that I became, but I knew that I needed a variety of experiences to really spread my wings and become the teacher I was meant to be. So I moved to Inman, KS.

Whether you're from Kansas or not, there's a pretty good chance you've never heard of Inman, but if you Google it, you'll learn that it's a tiny little town almost in the geographical center of the United States. When I got there, I found lush fields of wheat and corn that provide the financial backbone of the area, but I also found good people and an attractive small town lifestyle that have kept me there ever since. So I was the art teacher there as my second job in the teaching world, and I spent my summer preparing for my new classes, but I was also painting houses because that's what teachers do. We paint houses in the summer to make extra money. I didn't mind painting houses, and without that extra summer job, we would have been short on cash, and I would have never met Harvey.

When I first saw Harvey, he was a beautiful multi-colored caterpillar on a plant near the house I was painting. I was mesmerized by his vibrant colors, and that attraction prompted me to put him in a jar and take him with me that day. It seemed natural that he would go along with me when school started in August. All the kids liked my caterpillar, and they were the ones who named him Harvey. We provided all the comforts of home that the class caterpillar could ever want: a leaf and a stick inside his jar! Life was good for Harvey, and one Monday morning we noticed that over the weekend he had done what all caterpillars do by forming a chrysalis. I took the opportunity to teach a little science and said, "Hey guys, this is going to be a marvelous process. Harvey is going to emerge and become a butterfly!" In those pre-Google days, we didn't look up what kind of caterpillar he had been so we had no idea what kind of butterfly he was going to be.

He emerged over a weekend, a swallowtail butterfly with what would have been beautiful wings if not for the fact that he didn't have enough room in the jar to fully extend his wings, and they hardened all curled up. When the kids saw him, they were all sad, and I felt terrible! I had deformed Harvey by putting him in a jar that was too small. I tried to make amends to Harvey by bringing him home and feeding him sugar water in a spoon. When I took him out of his jar, he was able to walk around the table, but those gnarled wings would never allow him to fly. We all loved Harvey even though we knew his lifespan wasn't going be terribly long. However, I was determined to keep him alive and give him the best quality of life possible because I felt so guilty about what I had done.

One night about dusk, Michele and I were walking the dogs in the back of our property, and we came across a dead monarch butterfly. I picked up the monarch butterfly, looked at it for a minute and said to my wife, "I think I can put these wings on Harvey." She looked at me like a villager who just realized that Dr. Frankenstein had created a monster. Before she could respond I said, "I think that I can do it. I really do!" Now, one of the wings was a bit tattered, but most of it was there so I took the dead butterfly home and prepared for the transplant.

I originally thought I would anesthetize Harvey with alcohol, but I was afraid I might kill him so I hoped that butterflies didn't register pain the same way humans do. The tools I used to make jewelry became my operating instruments, and once I had Harvey securely in place, I cut off his deformed wings. I know that sounds a bit macabre, even on a butterfly, but I left little nubs so I would have a base I could use to attach the monarch wings. I applied super glue with a needle, and painstakingly attached the four new wings to Harvey's body. I blew gently on the wings until they dried, and then it was show time.

I released Harvey from his restraints, and he immediately began to move his new wings. Up and down! Up and down! My wife and I stood there awestruck watching this amazing thing. I moved Harvey to the edge of the table, and he flew across the room. His longest flight was around 15 feet, probably because of the hole in one of the transplanted wings, but he could actually fly! I realize Harvey's response was instinctive, and I won't anthropomorphize his actions into courage or determination. However, the idea he represented inspired me to start writing a children's book called *The Monarch of Castletown* where a young girl saves a butterfly the same way I saved Harvey, and in the process she learns about overcoming adversity, facing your fears, and emerging as a new, but equally beautiful creature.

Harvey has been gone for many years now, but the lesson he taught me endures. Whenever I face a new challenge, I know all I have to do is stand on the edge and spread my wings.

You can watch a video of Harvey at https://youtu.be/e-5MaWq9dJk

Christmas Miracle

Christmas in the Honeycutt house was usually a very stressful time. My siblings and I wanted to be excited, but we understood the realities of poverty. Our parents wanted to give us the same experience our friends had, but they knew that was impossible. The dissonance that was created when our expectations collided with our reality put everyone on edge from Thanksgiving until December 26th. One Christmas in Pomona, KS stands out in my memory, not because of the things we lacked, but because of the Christmas Miracle we received.

This particular Christmas was bleaker than usual. I hoped for presents but didn't really expect any when we barely had enough food on the table to feed everyone at most meals. When you go to bed hungry, you don't dream of toy trucks and action heroes, but our dire circumstances hadn't gone unnoticed. Our Christmas was about to be saved by the most unlikely of benefactors.

Our neighbors, Ken and Ann White, didn't have much more than we did, but Ken had a steady paycheck from the local quarry. This fact alone put them a step above us on the poverty scale, but it certainly didn't put them into the income bracket that we typically think of when we hear the word philanthropist.

One evening I looked out the window to see if the snow had stopped falling, and I noticed a sack on the porch. I opened the door and discovered it was full of groceries. No one had knocked on the door so it was obvious that the donor wanted to remain anonymous. I slipped on my coat and shoes and followed the tracks in the snow to Ken and Ann's house. I stood outside their modest home marveling at how two people with so little to give could generously share with us so we could have a wonderful Christmas dinner.

I walked slowly back to the house and brought the sack of groceries inside. I never told anyone where they came from because our neighbors didn't need any recognition or thanks. On that cold, dark December evening, I realized the positive effect of surrounding yourself with people like Ken and Ann, but I also learned the importance of being that kind of person myself. As I grew older, I looked for opportunities to offer a helping hand to others whenever I could because I never forgot the power of that Christmas Miracle.

The Wiffle Bat

Children in dysfunctional families use any means at their disposal to survive. Some withdraw while others use anger and misbehavior to feel in control of the chaos around them. I personally employed different tactics at different times, depending on the situation. This is only a guess on my part, but I'm betting my siblings and I are the only ones who ever used a wiffle bat to gain control of a dangerous situation.

When we were in Daytona Beach, Florida, we lived in some pretty unsavory neighborhoods. We never went out alone after dark, but on one particular night, we weren't safe inside our house. Dad went out drinking with a friend and left the five of us to fend for ourselves. Unfortunately, while he was gone, a man tried to break into our trailer.

Trailer houses back in the 1970s weren't very substantial when they were brand new. The one we were living in was hardly fit for human inhabitants so it is highly probable that the man who tried to rip off our back door would have succeeded eventually if we hadn't fought back. By the time we heard the noise and got to the back door, the would-be intruder already had the corner of the door bent up far enough that he was trying to crawl inside.

I'm sure there were knives in the kitchen and guns in the bedroom, but the closest item at hand was a wiffle bat so that became our weapon of choice. I doubt that the sting of a child's plastic toy had much effect as we pounded on the arm that stuck through the gaping hole. It's much more likely that the deterrent was five children screaming and snarling like a pack of Rottweilers. We weren't cowering in a corner whimpering. We meant business, and we weren't going down without a fight.

I might not have realized it at the time, but this was a great lesson on the importance of teamwork. We had a common goal, and everyone was an active participant in the endeavor. I also learned to attack every project or problem with passion, using all available resources, even if all I have is a wiffle bat.

Who Has Your Back

Never underestimate the importance of having people you can depend on in your life. As a child, I only had one person I could rely on. Dad was so undependable that we all knew Mom was the only thing holding the family together, but I had no idea what we could all endure as long as she had our backs.

Mom and Dad fought a lot so the abuse had to be pretty bad for her to leave, but occasionally it reached that level. This particular time she called some of Dad's relatives to help us gather a few meager belongings and head out. Calling on his family for help was a pretty risky move because poor families have an interesting dynamic. Someone who is a staunch supporter one minute can turn into your worst enemy the next. Unfortunately, that's exactly what happened.

Once these "caring" family members had us out in the middle of nowhere, the two of them beat my mother and stole her car. I don't recall an argument so I can only assume that this was the plan all along, but one thing I know for sure is that my mother was kicked to the ground as she fought to get back in the car.

If Mom cried or cursed her assailants, I don't remember it. All I remember is the six of us walking down the road together carrying our things. I'm not sure how far we walked, but in my mind I clearly see the abandoned farmhouse we found. Somehow, without saying a word, Mom communicated that we were home.

It was a very dark time in my life with only enough staples to keep us from starving. Mom found work nearby and did her best to provide enough to keep us going. We all pitched in and did what we could to help, but it was Mom who made our misery bearable. Eventually Mom reconciled with Dad and my journey continued, but now I knew that I could survive with almost nothing as long as I had someone like Mom who had my back.

What Did You Say

At one point in our nomadic life, my family ended up in a trailer park outside of Texarkana called Victory City. I can't begin to explain the irony of this name, but let's say that nobody living there was experiencing a victory of any kind. However, this was the place where I learned one of the most important lessons of my life—the power of words.

My dad was a racist so he said words that no one should ever speak, and he used his words to degrade and humiliate people. Since that was the common language in our house, I learned to use it, too. When you are raised this way, it takes a long time to unlearn this stuff, but I knew I had to if I wanted to build a life in mainstream, polite society.

The incident that started me on my road to verbal recovery involved our next-door neighbor who had a serious speech impediment along with some other cognitive challenges. When the neighbor would visit, the conversation usually contained an outrageous statement by my dad designed to get the neighbor to exclaim, "Good God, Carl." However, his disability changed the expression to, "Dood Dod, Dar." Then Dad would come home laughing and repeating, "Dood Dod, Dar" with ridicule and disdain for the neighbor. After dozens of times hearing this expression, I began repeating the phrase in the same mocking, derisive tone Dad always used.

One afternoon I started repeating "Dood Dod, Dar" over and over again near my bedroom window. I don't know why I did it, but I said it loudly enough that the neighbor heard me. He got very angry and came to the house to tell Dad what I was doing. My mindless recitation was interrupted by Dad yelling, "Kevin, get in here!" I could tell by their expressions I was in trouble, and somehow I knew the reason why.

"What did you say," Dad demanded.

"Dad, I just…"

"Shut up! What did you say?" he repeated.

"I was only…"

"Shut up. What did you say?" he queried once again.

It was clear that Dad wasn't going to take any responsibility for indoctrinating his kids into prejudice and making fun of others. I had to apologize and wear the full heat of that shame and humiliation by myself. That moment impacted me deeply, and I would recall every detail anytime I found myself tempted to make fun of others.

I tried to ease my conscience over the years by saying that I was just a kid, and I didn't know what I was doing. But not knowing is never an excuse for hurting someone else. Now I try to be cognizant of the way people feel, and focus on only the positive things in others because you don't build up your own life by tearing down someone else's with the things you say.

An Ode to Sandra Martin

I struggled with low self-esteem throughout my childhood. It's hard to believe in yourself when no one else does. I always felt love and support from my mom, but Moms are supposed to do that. I never had her obligatory faith in me validated by an independent second party until I met Sandra Martin.

We moved from Tennessee to New Oxford, Pennsylvania when I was in junior high school. As I got older, adjusting to our many moves became more difficult. My schoolwork seemed harder, and my clothes seemed shabbier so I was struggling academically as well as socially. Just when my world seemed bleaker than it ever had, I met a teacher who changed the course of my life.

Sandra Martin wasn't my teacher, but I passed her classroom every day when I entered the school, and she was always standing outside her door. At first we just said, "Hello," but gradually our conversations blossomed until she was someone I looked forward to spending a few minutes with every morning. One day she mentioned the upcoming school play she was casting and suggested that I try out. I had never participated in any school activities before because of the cost, but this was free so I took the letter home to show Mom. She gave her permission, and I auditioned for "A Deputy for Broken Bow." To my utter amazement, I got the lead. I was the Deputy!

Being a part of a theatrical community, even in junior high school, felt like home. It was okay to have shabby clothes and be different because I could pretend that was a choice. That was my character for the day. I poured my heart and soul into rehearsals, and I was ready for opening night. When the auditorium lights came on after the performance, I saw my dad in the audience with a look on his face I'd never seen before—a look of pride. I was hooked! I even went to college on an art and theater scholarship.

I look back on that first show and wonder where I would be today without that opportunity. I don't know if Mrs. Martin saw some potential in me that might improve the performance or if she just saw a lost, lonely boy who desperately needed to belong somewhere. Her motive doesn't matter, but every time I give a keynote speech in front of thousands of people, I know I'm there because of one teacher who believed in me.

Wrong Room, Right Person

My grandfather, Harry Smith, was a hard man, and he was intimidating to me as a child. As he got older, the edge came off, and I was able to relate to him and appreciate who he was as an artist and a human being. Unfortunately, about the time we started to get close, he developed emphysema, and his health continued to deteriorate until he entered the veterans' hospital in Topeka, KS. He was hooked up to a breathing machine, which made it difficult to converse, but the family still visited him regularly, and I know he appreciated having all of us there. On one of my last visits to the hospital, a nurse mistakenly sent me to the wrong room, and I became the right person for Harry Smith in a way I never imagined possible.

The day before I went to visit, Grandpa had a biopsy, and it didn't go well. Because of the complications, they had to move him to another room. When I arrived at the hospital, I told the nurse I was there to see Harry Smith. She exclaimed, "Oh, he'll be so happy. He hasn't had a visitor in so long!" I was trying to make sense of her comment because I had just been there last week when she ushered me into the room. I was greeted by a booming voice that said, "Bring him in!" I could tell the man in the bed was really, really happy to see me, and I could also tell he really, really wasn't my grandpa. He was a stranger named Harry Smith who hadn't had a visitor for a long time, and he still didn't. I wasn't sure what to do so I chose to visit with this other Harry Smith for an hour while my grandpa lay dying in another room.

I felt guilty for abandoning my grandpa for a long time, but this Harry Smith had no one, and my grandpa had a room full of family members to support him. Ultimately, I knew I'd made the correct choice. I might have been in the wrong room, but I was visiting with the right person.

Mad as a Hornet

Apparently paying bills and raising five children didn't cause enough stress for Dad because he would often create problems where none actually existed. A perfect example of how he would go looking for trouble occurred the day he decided to attack the hornets that built a nest in a tree outside our house. Now I'm not saying hornets outside your door is a thing to be desired, but none of us had been stung, and the hornets seemed to have a "live and let live" attitude toward us. None of that mattered to Dad once he decided they had to go.

Dad was a smart man, but he rarely applied his intellect to any of life's obstacles. I'm not sure why he failed to develop a plan or consider all possible outcomes, but dragging out his shotgun seemed to be his default solution to most problems. Even though this could be quite dangerous, his crazy antics also proved highly entertaining. On this particular occasion, we all hid in the relative safety of the house and watched out the window. Dad took careful aim, squeezed the trigger on his sawed-off shotgun, and promptly shot the branch in two that held the hornets' nest.

The shot resulted in a nest of angry hornets being deposited at Dad's feet. As the swarm stung him repeatedly, he did what I came to call the Happy Hornet Dance, which meant he ran around in circles like a scene from Benny Hill. We all had a good laugh, and I learned not to look for trouble, especially when you don't have a plan of attack or a reason to fight.

Who Are You

Everyone needs an identity. If kids don't have help finding a positive one, they may find a negative identity such as a gang affiliation, a reputation as a bully, or something even worse. As a child, I struggled for a long time to find my identity. Fortunately, I inherited my grandfather's artistic ability, and he fostered my interest by giving me art books and drawing pencils. It didn't take long before I was a better artist than my peers so each time we moved, I looked for opportunities to display my talent. Even if the other kids didn't know my name, I would hear them say, "That kid can draw!" That kind of positive feedback made it easy for me to know at last who I was. I was an artist!

I always encourage parents and teachers to help kids find what makes them special. Sometimes young people don't realize they are good at something until someone tells them. It sounds a little crazy, but it's true. If we can give them something to feel good about and take pride in, then they will develop the strength and self-confidence they need to resist less desirable identity choices. Once they've found that special talent, they can take it with them wherever they go in life.

I also encourage adults to continue developing new abilities. Never stop learning and growing. I didn't stop at drawing. I'm good, not great, at many things, and every new talent has served me well. Continue to find out who you are every day.

Pick and Choose

A big part of my life was spent in the company of dangerous people because Dad took us to the places frequented by dangerous people. For some reason he seemed to collect them or they were drawn to him. Part of growing up was realizing that I couldn't associate with these people. This was not a value judgment on my part; this was common sense. These people lived in a constant state of crisis. These people were always involved in some kind of drama. These people often went to jail. So when I finally got to the place where I could pick and choose the life I wanted, I knew I had to dissociate myself from these kinds of people.

This was definitely a hard decision to make and even harder to implement. When you come from poverty, no matter how difficult your life is, it is the life you know and you are comfortable with it. You know how to navigate the pitfalls. So change, even change for the better, is a challenging process, especially when the change involves leaving behind many of the people you know. When you don't know what will happen next and you have no way to picture a different future that feels safe, you will run back to what you know a million times. I've watched people run back to abusive relationships over and over. As bad as the relationships are, they know what to expect. In a way, bad relationships are more comfortable than the unknown.

I know how hard change can be, not only from my struggle, but what I saw my mother go through. She tried to leave my dad three different times, and circumstances kept pushing her back. The first time her car was stolen, and she was beaten and threatened by the perpetrators so she had no choice but to call Dad to come get us. The second time we were evicted from our house in the middle of the night after the money ran out. Mom had sold her car to help her parents, so once again she had no options. The last time she tried to leave, she paid her parents to watch us while she worked, but Grandma turned her in as an unfit mother. She had to go back with Dad to prove we could function as a family so she could get us out of the foster home. With no money, no car, and no family to help, she was forced to go back. There was something selfless about her tenacity, and she chose to endure suffering to preserve the family. Breaking free from the past is never easy, but perseverance and believing in your own ability are the keys to implementing the changes we need to make to find a better life.

My wife helped me tremendously when it came time to clean the closet of my life. I finally decided I had to get rid of the relationships in my life that weren't going anywhere. Many of them were co-dependent relationships that were wasting time—my time and theirs. What she helped me realize was the addiction I had to helping others, whether they deserved it or not. That might sound harsh, but many of the people in my life weren't interested in helping themselves. It made me feel good to help people, and I'm sure it felt good for them to receive help, but over time I learned that merely giving something to someone didn't really help them. Think about the poor people who win the lottery and are broke within a few years.

With our limited resources, both financial and physical, we all need to pick and choose the people we help. I don't know how many heartbeats I have, but I no longer waste them on people who aren't willing to help themselves. So be careful when you pick your closest friends and family because you only get one life, and you want to choose wisely.

We'll Laugh about This Some Day

Most of Dad's decisions can be classified in one of three ways: dangerous, illegal, or inappropriate. Sometimes they were all three, but his escapades were often tinged with humor from the sheer absurdity of his choices. I must admit the humor wasn't always immediately apparent, but sometimes the laughter and manic relief he provided were the only things that got us through the stress of our daily lives. If we didn't laugh immediately, we were pretty sure we would laugh about these things some day.

One such incident occurred in our house in Texarkana, Texas. Leon Butner owned the house, and he really didn't want to rent it because it was in such bad shape, but Dad convinced him he could fix the crumbling chimney and eliminate the snakes, spiders, and rats that had taken up residence since the house had been abandoned. Once Dad repaired the chimney and painted the house, it was actually one of the nicer places we lived. The only promise he didn't follow through on was eliminating the rats. We cohabited with them much to Dad's chagrin.

One evening as we were watching television, a rat casually walked through the kitchen and stopped by the stove. Without weighing any other options, Dad said, "Get my shotgun." Dad put a shell into the gun, took careful aim, and shot holes in the floor and the stove. Unfortunately, he completely missed the rat, but instead of scurrying away as expected, the rat launched a full frontal assault on his enemy running right up Dad's pant leg. Dad grabbed the rat just short of his groin and finally dispatched the vermin.

Now let me recap this event for you. A shotgun had been fired inside our house in close proximity to five children. The ensuing blast ripped a hole in the floor of the kitchen and the stove. A rat attacked Dad, and he killed it by crushing it with his bare hands. And we all started laughing. The sense of humor you develop when you have nothing else to sustain you is more valuable than people realize. I think finding the humor in many of my childhood experiences has helped me heal and move forward to find a better life.

A Deal with the Devil

We all give into temptations every day. Some are minor fails—cheating on our diet or doing personal business during working hours. Others are more serious ones—cheating on a spouse or failing to report income to the IRS. One important aspect of building a better life is developing a moral compass that helps you navigate the pitfalls everyone encounters. Without a personal North Star to guide you, wants can seem like needs, the end can justify the means, and a deal with the Devil feels acceptable.

I learned this lesson like I learned most things—the hard way. It all happened while I was rebuilding my beloved '69 Camaro. Even though I was doing all the body and interior work myself, I spent most of my money because parts were so expensive. A solution presented itself in the form of a kid whose family moved in just a few trailers down from us. This kid told me his brother worked in an auto parts store in Topeka, and he could get parts that he would sell to me at a huge discount because he would steal them from his employer. This was a real moral dilemma because I would never steal anything, but if I agreed to this, I would be paying his brother to steal for me.

Reluctantly, I agreed to the plan, and gave the kid every nickel I could scrape together. I was immediately filled with remorse. I knew I had made a terrible decision, but I didn't have any way to kill the deal. I tossed and turned in bed that night trying to figure a way out. Fortunately for me, the neighbor was an impressive liar and a cheat. The "deal" was a scam, and the parts never materialized. I was so relieved that I never mentioned the fact that he had stolen my money, especially since his family was so unpredictable that it would have been dangerous to ask for my money back. Some lessons come with a pretty high price tag, but in this case it was worth every penny I had to learn a valuable life lesson and avoid a deal with the Devil.

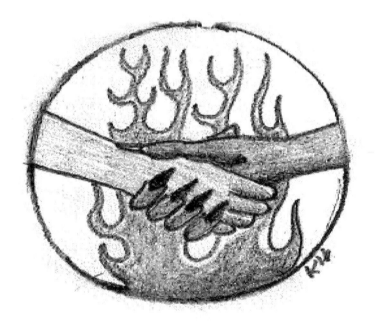

Follow the Rules

I wish I could say that I learned my lessons from Dad so well that I never made the same mistakes he did, but that wouldn't be the truth. I would do the same things he did and usually get a painful reminder of the right way to live my life. I was never the rule breaker he was, but occasionally I would take a shortcut like I did when I was the artist in residence for the five elementary schools in the Ottawa, KS school district. This wasn't the only time I chose to disregard the rules, but it was certainly the most memorable.

I started doing motivational talks with students about setting goals and never giving up. Because of my experience with karate, I knew how to break blocks of wood and stone, and that was always a dramatic way to end my presentations. I would tell the kids to never give up on their dreams because with determination, anything is possible. Then I'd do a two-knuckle punch that shattered the blocks to the delight of my audience. That's how it always worked. Well, that's how it worked when I followed the rules.

On the way to one presentation, I stopped by the lumberyard to pick up the patio stones I used for my big finale, but they were out. The only thing they had was something called chimney block. Instead of taking the time to go to another lumberyard to get the right product, I took a shortcut and loaded up the chimney block because I was short on time. I had no way of knowing that chimney block was much denser than the patio stones. I didn't plan ahead so I had no other option.

My presentation went very well, and I got to the point in the program where I said, "Don't give up, don't let anything stop you, just push right through," and I did my two-knuckle punch straight down with everything I had, and the block didn't break but my hand did. My hand immediately went numb so I didn't realize it was broken. Unwilling to fail in front of all of these students and teachers, I tried again. "Never let anything stop you," I shouted using my fist as a hammer in another attempt to break the blocks. "Even if you have to try over and over, don't let anything stop you," I yelled for the third time. To everyone's horror, the cloth protecting my hand from the surface of the chimney block had shifted slightly, and my broken hand split open and started bleeding in front of 300 terrified, traumatized elementary students. I looked at their wide eyes and open mouths and realized I had done this.

I put my bloody stump in my pocket, exited the building as quickly as I could, and drove my motorcycle home with one hand. The doctor put a cast on my hand so I had a painful reminder of my humiliation for several weeks as I tried to teach art with one hand. Thinking back over that experience, I realized I had failed because I tried to change the rules. I didn't make sure I had the right bricks I was used to working with, and you can't guarantee success if you don't follow the rules. The next time I did a presentation where I broke blocks, I made sure I had patio stone, but I was still pretty nervous. I brought my hand down with such force that the blocks shattered and flew all over the stage. My vindication was sweet, but that was the last time I broke blocks with any part of my body.

You Have Chosen Wisely

Choosing a life partner is probably the single most important decision anyone makes in his or her adult life. I've seen so many successful marriages where the couple works as a team using their individual talents to support and complement the other. Unfortunately, I've also seen too many marriages that were just the opposite. Anyone who knows me will attest to the fact that I won the spousal lottery. My friend, Terri Peckham, says that marriage is like buying a used car. You never know for sure what you're getting until you've driven it a while. If that's the case, I got a sleek roadster, and my wife got a clunker with a blown engine and some much needed bodywork. She's had me up on blocks for enough years that I hope she's finally starting to believe that she chose wisely.

I had so many things wrong with me when Michele and I got married. I knew the example my dad set for me was wrong, but it was the one I saw every day. When we fought in my family, we didn't use kid gloves; we fought to win. We scorched the earth with the vicious things we said, and that's how I fought with Michele. As you can imagine, I made her cry often in the early years of our marriage. She didn't know it at the time, but those tears were washing away the corrosion on my soul. It was a bill she didn't owe, but she paid it anyway. I'm still a work in progress, but I plan to spend the rest of my life trying to be worthy of her love and the life we've built together.

Benjamin and Gibson

Even though I had a less than idyllic childhood, my good fortune in matrimony has more than made up for my difficult start in life. Michele has been my rock and my inspiration as I've worked to become a better person. As educators, we've both worked hard to make the world a better place for children. Together we raised one son, Benjamin, and he's close to achieving his dream of becoming a teacher. He's also an author and a humanitarian who is making the world a better place in ways I could never imagine. There are many more things I could say about Ben, but he can tell his own story much better than I ever could.

When Ben left for college, Michele struggled with "empty nest syndrome" more than I did, but I knew that eventually she would realize that just the two of us together could be a good thing. We went to a few concerts, bought a couple of cars that most teenagers would covet, acquired a chair and half we could sit in together and watch Netflix, and started enjoying the freedom that comes once you are finished raising your children. All things considered, I was pretty happy with how our life was shaping up.

One night as I was sitting at the kitchen table, Michele came in carrying a white, plastic thing I hadn't seen in over 22 years, and she showed me the two lines in the little window. She said, "We're back in the game." I said, "I wasn't aware we still had any eligibility left." I quickly recovered and gave the correct response, "Yea!" Approximately eight months later, Gibson Lee Honeycutt came into our lives, and at age 48, I was back in the game big time. I think Gibson's arrival may be the universe saying, "If you are going to talk about raising kids, we're going to give you a fresh one so you can prove this stuff works." So my midnight run continues, but it's no longer a chaotic dash to parts unknown. Instead, it's a slow and steady climb to the top with a road map and a plan. I've taken all those lessons learned in all those towns that dot the landscape of my childhood, and I'm using them to heal, to forgive, and to help others. Michele and I will continue to learn and grow and provide the best life possible for this new miracle that has blessed our lives, and I pray for safe travels for all of us.

Made in the USA
Middletown, DE
04 August 2017